The Mafia Cookbook

Joseph "Joe Dogs" Iannuzzi

Simon & Schuster

New York London Toronto Sydney Tokyo Singapore

SIMON & SCHUSTER
Simon & Schuster Building
Rockefeller Center
1230 Avenue of the Americas
New York, New York 10020

The stories in the book are based on real events. In
some instances, dates, names, places, and other
details were changed to accommodate my recipes.–J.I.

DESIGNED BY BARBARA MARKS
Manufactured in the United States of America

10 9 8 7 6 5 4 3 2 1

Library of Congress Cataloging-in-Publication Data

Iannuzzi, Joseph.
    The Mafia cookbook / Joseph "Joe Dogs" Iannuzzi.
        p.   cm.
    Includes index.
        1. Cookery, Italian   2. Cookery, International. 3. Mafia—
    United States.   I. Title.
TX723.142   1993
641.5945—dc20   93-13520
                                                          CIP

ISBN: 0-671-86925-6

To my best female friend
LORRETTA

THIS BOOK IS DEDICATED TO MY
GOOD FRIEND AND *COMPARE* TOMMY AGRO . . .
WITHOUT YOU, THIS BOOK WOULD NOT BE
POSSIBLE.
REST IN PIECES.

THANK YOU MARILYN RITZ
FOR WALKING INTO THE KITCHEN OF
DON'S ITALIAN RESTAURANT
ON SINGER ISLAND, FLORIDA, ON
JANUARY 19, 1981, AND SAVING MY LIFE.
THANKS A MILLION.

—JOE DOGS

Recipes

Introduction

❦

I like to cook. I've always liked to cook. That is, as long as I didn't have to cook, I liked it. It was when I was made to cook I hated it, because if I didn't do it they'd either fire me or, later, fire at me.

I learned the hard way. How to cook, that is. When I was a kid my stepfather kicked me out of the house. He was an Irish bastard. So I had to learn quick. You follow me? I think I was thirty-eight or thirty-nine years old when that Irish _____ told me to cop a walk. Just kidding. I was fifteen years old. So I bounced around the pool halls until I was old enough to join the army. I was a GFU (General Flake-Up), so I was constantly on KP. The mess sergeant went out of his way to show me different recipes to cook and bake. Not because he was such a nice and generous guy. Because he was a fat lazy SOB who wanted me to learn so he could laze around on his fat ass all day.

After the army I got married and divorced and married and divorced and, in the early fifties, somehow found myself in Cleveland, Ohio. I needed a job, so I applied for work in one of the classiest restaurants in Cleveland. The chef who interviewed me laughed like hell when I told him my references and experiences. "Joey," the chef said, "if you promise me to forget everything you've learned about cooking I'll give you a job." *Voilà!* I was in. The kitchen. As a saucier.

I learned how to make soups and sauces, and experimented

cooking with brandies and different wines. After six months I figured I had the experience to cook anywhere, even the Big Apple,
my hometown. So I stole another car and drove back to New York.
(I couldn't very well drive the stolen car that had taken me to
Ohio back to New York.) Back in New York: another marriage,
another divorce. Oh-for-three.

Anyway, I worked in different diners and restaurants around
New York, cooking food and making book. Through my bookmaking partners I got an application to join a very exclusive
club: the Mothers And Fathers Italian Association. MAFIA, for
short. Normally you needed a college degree to be accepted, as
there were some very intelligent guys in this club. Some could
almost read and write. But they let me slide into their club
because of my cooking. They said they would "learn" me the
rules and regulations as time went on.

Now, mobsters love to eat. They eat while planning crimes
and they eat after committing crimes, and when there are no
crimes, they eat while waiting for them to happen. And mobsters
are very picky. They know what they like, and when they like it
they eat all of it. And then more. Look at the stomachs on these
guys the next time television shows one of them being escorted
into court in handcuffs. These are some very serious eaters.

Which is why some of these recipes call for such heavy
sauces. Remember the crowd I was feeding—any meal may be
their last, so it better be a good one. Crime may not pay, but it
sure gives you a hell of an appetite.

So don't be scared off by the butter and cream. Just serve the
richer sauces on the side instead of dumping them on top of the
food.

My cooking for my mentor, my rabbi, my *compare*, Tommy

Agro, came in very handy, as T.A. was constantly on the lam. Tommy A. and his crew were forever traveling to different apartments in different states to lay low, and we'd always leave in a rush and I wouldn't even get to pack up my pots and pans and knives. "Leave them, Joey" was T.A.'s familiar refrain. "We'll buy new ones." Despite  these culinary hardships, lamming it was a good experience. I was perfecting my craft.

The members of my new club ate a lot of veal and an awful lot of pasta. But that didn't stop me from experimenting with dishes. I'd never tell the crew what I was cooking if it wasn't a recipe from the old country. They wouldn't have eaten it (and they might have shot me). But once they were licking their chops, I'd let them in on the fact that they were wolfing down Mandarin Pork Roast, or Steak au Poivre, and I never received a complaint.

I cooked for the club—among other jobs—for about ten years. Then I had a terrible accident. I kept walking into this baseball bat and this iron pipe. Some of my pals were trying to see if my head was harder than those two instruments. It was, just barely. But because of this experience I was enticed to join another club on a sort of double-secret probation. This club was called the Full-Blooded Italians, or, for short, FBI. The guys in my new club asked me to spy on the guys in my old club who had tried to kill me. I had no problem with that. Revenge, like my Cicoria Insalata, is best eaten cold.

When it came to food, the members of my new club were no

different from the members of my old club. They all ate like they were going to the chair. You don't have to eat that way with the recipes in this book. You just have to enjoy them. Because they've been tested on the worst of the worst and the best of the best. And they've all passed with flying colors.

Mangia! Buon appetito!

—Joe Dogs

Menu

Pasta Marinara
Veal Marsala

HALLANDALE, FLORIDA, 1974
TOMMY AGRO'S APARTMENT

PEOPLE PRESENT:
Joe Dogs
Tommy "T.A." Agro (Gambino soldier)
Louie Esposito
Skinny Bobby DeSimone
Buzzy Faldo (Gambino Associates; T.A.'s Florida crew)

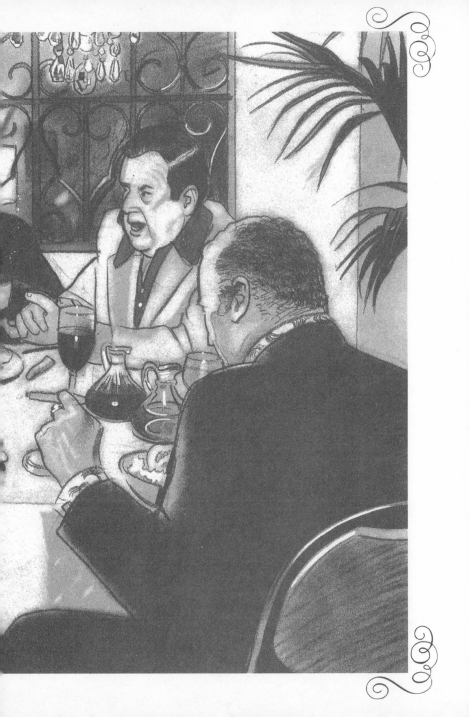

ommy Agro was down from New York, on the lam from an extortion bit handed up by a federal grand jury. I didn't find out how my *compares* always learned ahead of time about these so-called secret indictments until years later. Turns out they'd planted a mole in the U.S. Attorney's office, a secretary who typed up the paperwork, handed it to her boss, and immediately called the Gambinos with a warning.

Anyway, Tommy (aka T.A.) had blown town in a hurry, and he was nervous. And when T.A.—moody on a good day— was nervous, I liked to stay traditional. It only upset him more when I experimented in the kitchen. So veal and pasta were just the trick. Tommy sat down to a pinochle game with some of our south Florida Gambino crew—Louie Esposito, Skinny Bobby DeSimone, and Buzzy Faldo—while I headed for the stove to whip up a pot of my special marinara sauce. This is a classic. Just throw in a littl'a this, a littl'a that and you got a sauce to die for (you should pardon the expression).

Pasta Marinara

MARINARA SAUCE

> *2 cloves garlic, crushed and chopped fine*
> *¼ cup olive oil (extra-virgin or virgin preferred)*

1 (28-ounce) can peeled tomatoes (Progresso Pomodori
    Pelati con Basilico or Pope brand preferred),
    chopped fine
½ teaspoon garlic powder
¼ teaspoon dry mustard
¼ teaspoon pepper
2 tablespoons crushed dried basil
1 cup chicken stock

*I*n a small saucepan sauté garlic in olive oil until garlic dissolves (do not brown or burn). Add chopped tomatoes, stir, and simmer for 5 minutes. Add remaining ingredients, stir, and allow to simmer over low heat for approximately 25 to 30 minutes. Serve over your favorite pasta.

"Hey Joey," Tommy yelled from the living room while the sauce was simmering. "You didn't tell your wife that I'm here, did you? I don't want anybody to know I'm down here."

"Damn, Tommy, I wish you would have told me this before," I answered. Of course I hadn't told Bunny, but it was time to get Tommy's goat a little, loosen him up. "I already told her. In fact, I heard her telling her girlfriend Margie about you."

"Who the hell is Margie?" T.A. exploded. "Can't you guys do anything without reporting to your _____ing wives?"

"Oh, Margie, she's the girl who's married to the Florida State's Attorney," I answered. "I'm sure she'll tell her husband about you. She knows you're a Mafia guy."

"Joey, you get back in that kitchen before I eat your ____ing eyes for dinner."

Okay, Tom, the blue-plate eyeball special for you—everyone else gets the veal.

⚜

Veal Marsala

½ cup flour

1½ pounds veal (scaloppini cut), pounded thin with mallet

6 ounces (1½ sticks) butter, melted (clarified preferred)

¾ cup Florio sweet Marsala wine

2 ounces Grand Marnier

1 pound mushrooms, cleaned, sliced, and sautéed (see Note)

Juice of ½ lemon

¼ teaspoon white pepper

Flour veal on both sides. Heat butter in frying pan (do not burn). Shake off excess flour and sauté veal on both sides, lightly, over medium to low heat. Remove veal and set aside. Pour wine into saucepan and stir. Then add Grand Marnier, stir, and ignite to burn off alcohol. After flame dies, cook sauce until condensed to half the amount, put veal back in saucepan, and cook for another 5 minutes, stirring occasionally. Stir in the sautéed mushrooms, lemon juice and pepper and serve. *Serves 4 to 6.*

Note: To sauté mushrooms, clean and slice them and sauté them in ¼ pound melted butter. Add 2 ounces sweet sherry and cook over low flame for 20 minutes, stirring occasionally.

〰

"Joey, Joey, how do you get the sauce so sweet?" Skinny Bobby wanted to know.

"The Grand Marnier does it," I told him. "I burn out all the alcohol, though."

I sat back and watched everyone eat. They were gobbling up the food like it was their last meal. You would have thought they were all going to the chair. After dinner they all leaned back and made vulgar noises while I went to the kitchen to put coffee on.

"What the hell is this," I screamed, running out of the kitchen with a jar of pickles. Inside, nestled among the gherkins, was a human index finger. I threw it on the table and everyone started laughing.

"Oh, that's Frankie's finger," Tommy Agro said at last. "He used to tend bar for me. Whenever I open up a new joint I put that jar behind the bar, where all the people who work for me can see it. Then I put up a small sign that says, *This is Frankie's finger. It's here because he stole from his boss.* That way, any _____ who works for me will think twice before stealing. If I catch him a second time, they lose their hand. So far I got only one of those. It's home in my freezer in New York. Want me to bring it down next time I come, Joey?"

"*Marrone*, no!" I shook my head, and edged back into T.A.'s kitchen, on the lookout for any more body parts.

Menu

Monkfish Marinelli

HALLANDALE, FLORIDA, 1976
TOMMY AGRO'S APARTMENT

PEOPLE PRESENT:
Joe Dogs
Tommy Agro

I named this recipe in honor of a Colombo crime family soldier who used to pull B&Es with me up in Connecticut.
He was also a big fisherman, and taught me how to fillet a fish. I
usually only prepared this dish at home for me and my wife,
Bunny. But when Tommy Agro called about a week after he'd hit
town—still laying low in Florida—I decided to get a little daring.
By this time he'd calmed down a little, so when he ordered me to
get over to his apartment to cook dinner and discuss a race we
were planning to fix at Gulfstream Park, I stopped by a dockside
fishmonger on the way and picked up a fresh monkfish.

Monkfish Marinelli

¾ pound monkfish fillet
2 tablespoons olive oil (extra-virgin or virgin preferred)
⅓ cup flour
1 heaping tablespoon finely chopped garlic
¾ cup dry white wine
¼ pound (1 stick) butter
¼ cup chopped fresh parsley
Salt and pepper to taste
1 pound linguine

*C*ut monkfish into ½-inch-thick medallions. Heat olive oil in skillet. Dredge monkfish in flour (shake off excess). Sauté fish on both sides until golden brown. Stir in chopped garlic, add white wine, and simmer 5 minutes.

"So what's the chances of us getting double-banged on this race fix?" T.A. asked. He was nosing around the kitchen—bothering me—because there was no one else in the apartment to play pinochle with.

I explained to him for what must have been the hundredth time how I'd "reached" a crooked horse trainer named Sean O'Leary. Sean was a degenerate gambler, and he was into his shylock for close to 20 large. Unbeknownst to Sean, his shylock was in my crew. Anyway, Sean said that for around $15,000 in expense money up front he could get to four of the seven jocks in Saturday's sixth race at Gulfstream. That meant we only had to "wheel" the remaining three horses—all longshots—for a guar-

anteed winner. The split would be four ways: Me, T.A., Sean, and a Palm Beach bookmaker named Freddie Campo who I'd brought in to help me place the bets. In those days, the Florida tracks weren't computerized, and getting down, say, a $30,000 box at a betting window took a long time.

T.A. was satisfied with the setup, and pestered me to hurry up and finish cooking. Hey, Tommy, hold ya horses, will ya? I started the sauce to shut him up.

*A*dd butter to the simmering monkfish a little at a time. Then add chopped parsley, plus salt and pepper to taste. Cook pasta in 2 quarts salted water until *al dente*. Drain and place on platter, or individual plates. Place monkfish on pasta, and pour sauce from skillet over fish and pasta. *Serves 2.*

That Saturday the fix went down like a three-dollar fighter. Sean reached the jocks, who pulled the four favorites. Freddie Campo and I bet with both hands, each getting $15,000 down on longshot boxes. We took home $128,000. Subtracting the $30,000 we'd bet, and the $15,000 in "expenses," we'd cleared 83 large. Before the Gulfstream meet was over, our "consortium" had "won" approximately $800,000. I didn't know what I liked better, being a crook or being a cook.

Cicoria Insalata
(Dandelion Greens Salad)
Panacotte (Greens and Beans)

BROOKLYN, NEW YORK, 1975
LITTLE DOM CATALDO'S SAFE HOUSE

PEOPLE PRESENT:
Joe Dogs
Dominick "Little Dom" Cataldo (Colombo soldier and hitman)
Frank and Lino (Colombo associates, members of Little Dom's crew)

wo hours earlier, Little Dom Cataldo and I had been scrunched down in the front seat of his car, waiting for the carrier to come out of the loan office with the satchel. Little Dom was a soldier, and hitman, in the Colombo family. To look at him you'd never believe that the guy had murdered over ten people.

"I put him in Boot Hill" was one of Little Dom's favorite expressions. It wasn't brag. Just fact. Little Dom, who had a passing resemblance to the actor John Garfield, did have his own private burial grounds. A certain hill along the Taconic Parkway twenty miles or so north of New York City. But we hadn't capped anybody tonight. This had been a straight boost, $143,000 in drug money. The beauty part was, we'd ripped off another wiseguy whose capo had banned drug dealing. So who was the guy going to run to? Talk about your "no-fault" robberies.

Anyway, now we were back in Little Dom's safe house in Red Hook, Brooklyn, by the docks, divvying up the cash. It was me, Little Dom, and two of his crew, Frank and Lino. Everybody was hungry. Little Dom had told me he was tired of the "same old garbage." His heart was still racing, like it did whenever he nailed a big score, and he didn't want no meat. No problem. I decided on something light—a fresh salad with a nice vinaigrette and a vegetable casserole. As usual, his kitchen was stocked. The only thing I had to do was send Lino out for the dandelion greens.

Cicoria Insalata

1 bunch dandelion greens
½ cup olive oil (extra-virgin or virgin preferred)
1 teaspoon chopped garlic
1 tablespoon red wine vinegar (or lemon juice)
1 small red onion, sliced thin

*W*ash greens and pat dry. Add remaining ingredients to greens and toss thoroughly. Adjust seasoning to taste. *Serves 4.*

Panacotte (Greens and Beans)

1 head escarole
4 whole cloves garlic
2 tablespoons olive oil (extra-virgin or virgin preferred)
½ teaspoon crushed red pepper flakes (optional)
1 (16-ounce) can cannellini beans with juice (or
   approximately 1 cup dried beans, presoaked and
   cooked)
Salt and pepper to taste
2 cups cubed stale bread
½ cup freshly grated Parmesan cheese

*W*ash and tear escarole. Slowly sauté garlic cloves (whole) in olive oil. Remove frying pan from heat.

Allow to cool slightly. Add crushed red pepper and escarole and cook approximately 15 minutes over medium heat until tender. Add beans with juice and bring to boil. Taste for seasoning and add salt and pepper if needed. Put bread cubes in casserole dish with ¼ cup Parmesan cheese and escarole-and-bean mixture. Sprinkle remaining grated Parmesan (¼ cup) over top.

Bake in preheated 375-degree oven until slightly browned (approximately 20 minutes). Serve with crusty Italian bread, or Italian garlic bread, and wine. *Serves 4.*

"Joey, did I ever tell you about the time I popped that big fat Lucchese family guy?" Little Dom asked between delicious bites. "I hated this ____, he owed me vig for a long time, and I talked his own right-hand man, Johnny was his name, into conning him into meeting me in a parking lot in Queens.

"Anyway, after I whacked him, Johnny says to me, 'What're we gonna do with this fat pig now?' And since he got the guy there for me to whack, it's only fair I help him get rid of the body. So we stuff him into my trunk and drive to Boot Hill. I told Johnny that we gotta dig deep, five or six feet, 'cause the lime I use to cover the body smells, even through the ground. When we were finished, I drove my car as close as I could to the hole, and we threw the fat man in.

"Then I said, 'Damn, Johnny, I forgot to take his watch off, his ring and his dough. No sense in burying them.' So Johnny jumps in the hole to get the stuff and I shot him too. I put the lime in, then the dirt, then the grass seed. But I had a lot of dirt to spread around, because I had a two-story job there.

"Ha ha, that's funny, Joey. A two-story job."

Little Dom Cataldo cracked himself up.

Shrimp Scampi

NORTH MIAMI BEACH, FLORIDA, 1974
JIGGS FORLANO'S APARTMENT

PEOPLE PRESENT:
Joe Dogs
Tommy Agro
Jiggs Forlano (Colombo capo)
Bobby "Bobby Anthony" Amelio and Rabbit Fusco (drug dealers)

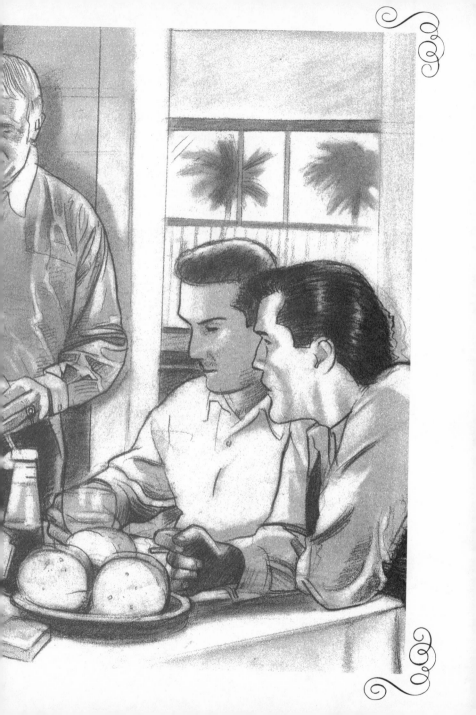

*J*iggs was a Colombo family capo from Brooklyn who liked to tell people he'd retired to Miami. Yeah. You retire from the mob when you retire from the living. It's like the IRA motto: "Once in, never out." Anyway, Jiggs had set up a meet with two suitcases from New York who needed investors in a marijuana-smuggling operation. He figured Tommy Agro could come with some fast cash. T.A. brought me to the meet as backup.

Bobby Amelio (aka Bobby Anthony) and his partner, Rabbit Fusco, were a couple of knockaround Mafia wannabes—babes in the woods, we called those kind—who were always on the fringe of a hustle. T.A. didn't like them, but "like" didn't matter to Tommy when money was involved. Jiggs made the introductions and began pouring drinks while I headed for the kitchen to impress the guys with my Shrimp Scampi. Now I know you're gonna say, Whoa, half a pound of butter and sour cream?! But remember, these guys ain't exactly concerned about their cholesterol count. So when serving guests with more normal appetites just keep the sauce on the side.

Shrimp Scampi

2 pounds jumbo shrimp (preferably under 15 to a
  pound)
½ pound (2 sticks) butter
1 shallot, chopped fine
3 cloves garlic, crushed and chopped fine
2 cups sour cream

2 tablespoons chopped dried chives
1 teaspoon garlic powder
¼ teaspoon white pepper
1 teaspoon Accent (optional)

*S*hell, devein, and butterfly shrimp. Set on large flat pan or large microwave dish. Set aside.

"What are you gonna cook for these guys, Joe? I didn't know you knew how to cook." Jiggs, a huge man with an Italian cigar nub apparently surgically attached to the side of his mouth, looked impressed.

"I used to be a sauce chef when I was a working stiff," I told him. "I like foolin' around in the kitchen."

"You mean you retired from workin' so you could become T.A.'s valet, chauffeur, and ____ing cook?" he asked. I lifted a large carving knife and Jiggs went back out to the living room while I went back to my shrimp.

*M*elt butter in a good, thick metal pot (do not scorch). Add chopped shallot and garlic, and sauté for 3 to 5 minutes over low heat. Add sour cream and stir. (It is thick at first, but once heated it will thin.) Add chives, garlic powder, pepper, and Accent, if using). Simmer over low heat, stirring occasionally, for approximately 30 to 45 minutes until it thickens to a nice texture.

"Jiggs, you staying for dinner?" I shouted.

"I'd like to, Joey, but you guys got business to attend to what I don't want to know about. I'm gonna take a walk."

*I*f you're going to broil the shrimp, watch them closely so they don't overcook. If you microwave them, do so for 3 to 3½ minutes on high setting. Pour sauce over shrimp and serve with rice. *Serves 4.*

"Joey, I never had shrimp scampi like this before," Rabbit Fusco said.

"Me either," Bobby Anthony agreed, licking his chops. "Now listen, we got a ton of that stuff coming in on the boat from Colombia. It'll be here in about ten days. I need some front money from you guys."

"How much do we have to come up with?" I asked.

"Fifteen grand."

"Marrone," T.A. whooshed. "And suppose I just hand youse this fifteen large? What's in it for me? I wasn't made with a finger, you know."

Menu

Baked Pork Chops
Philadelphia

WEST PALM BEACH, FLORIDA, 1975
MY HOME

PEOPLE PRESENT:
Joe Dogs
Tommy Agro

J invited Tommy Agro over to my house for dinner. I gave my wife, Bunny, who was also a good cook, the night off. Since the reefer smuggler Bobby Anthony (see Shrimp Scampi) never consummated his dope deal, Tommy shylocked out as a loan the $15,000 we had given him for the dope. But he'd been slow coming back with his payments. That extortion bit T.A.'d been dodging in New York looked like it was finally going to catch up with him, and he wanted to make contingency plans in case he had to go into the joint. This recipe is a man's-man kind of dinner I'd picked up from a Philly mobster vacationing in Miami, and I wanted to make this a special occasion, like a last meal, just in case I didn't see T.A. for a while.

Baked Pork Chops Philadelphia

2 tablespoons vegetable oil
4 pork chops (1 inch thick)
4 tablespoons (½ stick) butter
1 pound mushrooms, cleaned and sliced
2 shallots, grated or chopped very fine
Salt and pepper to taste
¼ cup cognac
¼ cup dry white wine
1½ tablespoons green peppercorns
1¼ cups heavy cream
1 tablespoon Accent (optional)

*H*eat vegetable oil in a fairly large saucepan. When hot, cook the pork chops for 3 minutes on each side to brown a little. Put pork aside. Add butter to pan and cook mushrooms and shallots for another 5 minutes. Season with salt and pepper. Then add cognac and wine and cook for another 4 minutes, stirring, over high heat. Mix peppercorns and cream in separate bowl. Crush peppercorns into cream. Add Accent. Pour mixture over mushrooms and shallots and simmer for 1 to 2 minutes, stirring occasionally.

From my living room, I heard the apoplectic T.A. yelling into the kitchen: "You tell this ____ Bobby Anthony that I want my ____ing money back. All of it. By no later than the first of the month. And I want a ten-grand bonus. You hear?"

*P*lace the pork chops in a baking pan. Pour the mushroom-shallot mixture over the pork. Cover and bake for 20 minutes in a preheated 350-degree oven. Serve with vegetable, potato, and applesauce.

"Joey, if I hafta go in and this guy don't deliver, I don't want you to do nothin'. I'll take care of this from the inside. I'll reach out for him. I need you out here watching my back. *Marrone*, what is this, Joey, pork? This is good. Ain't this what the Jews eat?"

"No, Tommy," I said. "Jewish people don't eat pork."

Menu

Mandarin Pork Roast
Rice and Ricotta Pudding

QUEENS, NEW YORK, 1976
UNDISCLOSED LOCATION

PEOPLE PRESENT:
Joe Dogs
Thomas DiBella (Boss, Colombo family)
Allie LaMonte (Colombo capo)
Dominick "Little Dom" Cataldo
assorted Colombo capos, soldiers, and associates

$\mathcal{T}$alk about a dangerous meal. Cooking for capos had always been nerve-racking enough. But Thomas DiBella had just been named acting head of the Colombo crime family while Carmine "Snake" Persico did a stretch in the federal pen. The Colombo *famiglia* were fêting the new boss with a round of dinners. When Little Dominick Cataldo's turn rolled around, he flew me up from Florida to put on the dog. (Ooh, I love a bad joke.) Little Dom owned a club in Queens—and he gave me free run of the kitchen.

Little Dom was nervous. He wanted everything to be just right. There were more than a dozen Colombo crew members present, each of them a heavyweight. "Please make everything perfect for the new Scoutmaster," Dom begged me. "And, Joey, please watch your mouth tonight. I know how you're always calling us wops, and I understand it's a joke. But please don't let none of those old zips hear you talkin' like that."

I promised to behave myself, and got to work on the pork.

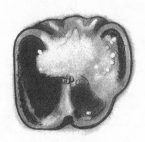

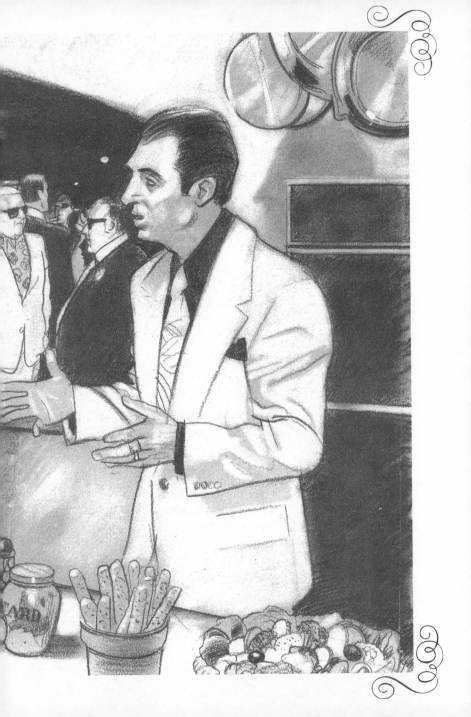

Mandarin Pork Roast

1 (6-pound) boneless pork loin (tied with string)
1 teaspoon salt
½ teaspoon white pepper
¾ teaspoon garlic powder
2¼ tablespoons Dijon mustard
1 (11-ounce) can mandarin oranges
¼ cup light brown sugar
¼ cup red wine vinegar
1 chicken bouillon cube
1¼ tablespoons soy sauce (low-salt)
2 tablespoons cornstarch
¾ cup water
1 medium onion, chopped
½ cup chopped green pepper

Trim excess fat from pork. Rub salt, pepper, and garlic powder into pork. Spread mustard over roast. Place roast in large dutch oven. Cover and bake in preheated 325-degree oven until meat thermometer reads 170 degrees (approximately 3 hours).

Drain oranges. Save liquid. Place orange liquid, brown sugar, vinegar, chicken bouillon cube, soy sauce, cornstarch, and water in saucepan. Cook, stirring, over medium heat until smooth and thickened. Remove from heat and stir in onion, green pepper, and oranges. Spoon sauce over roast and bake uncovered for 30 to 40 minutes, basting occasionally. Slice pork and serve with sauce. *Serves 14 to 16.*

I was allowed to dine with the Colombo boss and his soldiers—the only Gambino honored like that at the table. After dinner, DiBella came over, embraced me, and kissed me on both cheeks. (Don't get me wrong, we weren't fags or nothing. It was just our way of showing respect.)

"Joey, I want you to know how much I enjoyed that meal," the acting Don said to me. "I know it was some kind of southern dish, because Little Dom tells me you're from the south. So where exactly in South Brooklyn you from?"

I kid you not. The guy may have been a boss, but he was still a lob at heart. Now, a lot of the boys had brought dessert with them from a variety of Italian bakeries. But since this was Little Dom's "Scoutmaster," I really wanted to do it up. So before anyone could get to cutting open the store-bought desserts, I had the waiters bring out my famous Rice and Ricotta Pudding.

Rice and Ricotta Pudding

FILLING

> *4 cups whole-milk ricotta cheese (2 15-ounce containers; Polly-O brand preferred)*
> *1 cup sugar*
> *1 tablespoon grated lemon peel*
> *1 ounce semisweet chocolate, melted*

*B*eat ricotta and sugar (with electric beater) until creamy. Mix in lemon peel and chocolate. Set aside.

PUDDING

> *1⅛ cups rice*
> *6 cups milk*
> *¾ cup sugar*
> *3 eggs*
> *¾ teaspoon vanilla*
> *Butter for coating baking dish*
> *Flour for dusting*
> *1 tablespoon ground cinnamon*

*C*ombine rice, milk, and sugar in large saucepan. Bring to boil, uncovered, over low heat. Simmer, uncovered, for 20 minutes from boiling point, stirring frequently. Remove from heat. Reserve ¼ cup of rice pudding liquid (skimmed from top) in small bowl. Cool along with pudding for 20 minutes. Beat eggs and reserved liquid until blended (do not overbeat). Trickle into rice mixture, stirring well. Add vanilla. Generously butter a high, 12-inch round baking dish and dust with flour. Spread about half the pudding on bottom of baking dish. Spread ricotta cream filling over pudding and cover with remaining pudding. Bake in preheated 325-degree oven for 1 hour 15 minutes. Serve hot or cold, sprinkled with cinnamon.

Menu

New York Strip Steak Florentine with Sautéed Mushrooms Asparagus Hollandaise

HALLANDALE, FLORIDA, 1976
TOMMY AGRO'S APARTMENT

PEOPLE PRESENT:
Joe Dogs   Tommy Agro
Skinny Bobby DeSimone
Louie Esposito   Buzzy Faldo

It was T.A.'s coming-out party. He'd just done eight months—mostly in the hospital ward because of his asthma—and this was his first night back in Florida. He'd asked me, Skinny Bobby, Louie, and Buzzy over, and I'd told him his wish was my culinary command. Like any guy fresh from the joint, he wanted steak. (Tip for would-be *compares:* if any guy wants to join your crew and tells you he's just out of the joint, take him to dinner. If he orders anything but steak or lobster, he's lying and probably a Fed.)

⌘

New York Strip Steak Florentine with Sautéed Mushrooms

3½ tablespoons butter

2 teaspoons olive oil (extra-virgin or virgin preferred)

2 pounds mushrooms, cleaned and sliced

Salt and pepper to taste

2 tablespoons chopped fresh chives (or 1 tablespoon dried crushed chives)

3 tablespoons chopped fresh parsley

3 cloves garlic, sliced paper thin with single-edge razor blade or crushed and chopped fine

1 shallot, chopped fine

¼ cup cognac

Juice of ½ lemon

5 New York strip steaks, 8 ounces each

*H*eat butter and olive oil in large frying pan over medium to high heat. When hot, add mushrooms and 1 teaspoon salt and ½ teaspoon pepper. Cook for 10 minutes, stirring or tossing occasionally. Add chives, parsley, garlic, and shallot, stirring them in to blend for 7 or 8 more minutes. Then add cognac and lemon juice. Allow to simmer for 5 more minutes, stirring occasionally. Taste and check for seasoning. Broil steaks to your preference (rare preferred) and pour sautéed mushrooms over steaks. Mushroom recipe is for 5 steaks. I like to serve this with a nice asparagus in hollandaise sauce. Just serve the sauce on the side if it's too rich.

Asparagus Hollandaise

4 egg yolks
¼ teaspoon dry mustard
¼ teaspoon salt
¼ teaspoon white pepper
Juice of ½ lemon
½ pound (2 sticks) butter, melted and clarified by pouring off milky residue
1 bunch asparagus spears (approximately 20 stalks), trimmed and steamed

*P*lace egg yolks, mustard, salt, pepper, and lemon juice in blender and blend at high speed for 1 minute.

Then put on low speed and slowly add clarified butter until mixture thickens. *Very important:* Do not scorch butter, and pour only the clarified butter—not any milky residue—into blender. Pour over steamed asparagus stalks. *Serves 4.*

"Joey, these mushrooms are so good," Tommy said in the calmest voice I'd heard in years. The joint must have done him good.

"You gotta be careful with mushrooms, though, Tommy." Skinny Bobby always had to put in his two cents. "Some of them are poisonous."

"Yeah, I know," I said. "I lost my first wife that way."

Tommy was seriously taken aback. "Jeez, Joey, I didn't know that. You never said nuttin'."

By this time I was almost in tears. "Yeah, I lost my second wife, too. From a crushed skull."

"Marrone," T.A. said. "What happened? Car accident?"

"Nah . . . She wouldn't eat the poison mushrooms."

Menu

Manicotti Marinara with Mint

HALLANDALE, FLORIDA, 1976
TOMMY AGRO'S APARTMENT

PEOPLE PRESENT:
Joe Dogs
Tommy Agro
Skinny Bobby DeSimone
Louie Esposito
Buzzy Faldo

*T*here was a broad in Tommy's apartment this afternoon, and Tommy was always trying to show me off if he thought it would help get his worthless little ass in the sack. She said her name was Jennifer—Jenny, the crew started calling her—and I must admit, she was a looker. She'd shown up at the apartment peddling Stanley Products door-to-door. You know, shaving cream, toothpaste, razor blades, stuff like that. She had samples with her, and you'd order from her catalogue. Personally, I suspected she was a hooker with a great angle. No matter. It wasn't like any of us were averse to popping a hooker.

Anyway, right away T.A. starts in with his lord-of-the-manor routine. "Jenny, honey, I want you to meet my personal chef, Joey Dogs. You're gonna stay and have dinner with us, Jenny. What're you selling? *Marrone*, what a body you got there. You ain't selling that, are you? Ha ha. Just kidding. Joey, cook up something special for my little Princess Jenny here. Hurry up, Joey! Jenny's hungry!"

Like I need this, right? Tommy was making Skinny Bobby and Louie buy a lot of junk from Jenny when I left for the kitchen to whip up a little manicotti for her highness.

Manicotti Marinara with Mint

CREPES

> 1 cup flour
> 1 cup plus 2 tablespoons water
> 2 eggs

*B*eat flour, water, and eggs well to make batter. Pour, ⅛ cup at a time, into slightly heated and greased 9-inch frying pan (batter should make 8 to 10 thin crepes). Rotate frying pan to distribute batter evenly. Cook until bottom of crepe is just dry and crepe can be removed from frying pan with rubber spatula (top of crepe should remain moist). Lay crepes flat in clean work area until batter is used up.

"Yes, honey, put Bobby down for a case of shaving cream. Louie too." Tommy's largesse from the living room.

"But Tommy," Jenny protested, "there's twenty-four tubes to a case, at $4.95 a tube. That's a lot of money."

"Don't you worry, Jenny, honey, both these lobs shave two, sometimes three times a day. Right, boys?"

The crew muttered their assents as I snuck back into the kitchen, but not before I heard T.A. put me down for a case too.

Hey, it's only money, right? I began making the cheese filling for the manicotti.

CHEESE FILLING

> *1½ cups whole-milk ricotta cheese (Polly-O brand preferred)*
> *¼ pound mozzarella cheese, diced*
> *½ cup freshly grated Parmesan cheese*
> *12 to 15 fresh mint leaves, well chopped*
> *Salt and pepper to taste*
> *Marinara Sauce (see page 16)*

Mix the three cheeses, chopped mint leaves, and salt and pepper in a bowl. Spoon evenly into center of crepes. Roll crepes and fold the ends underneath, leaving seam on bottom. Spoon a few tablespoons of marinara sauce into bottom of casserole dish and spread evenly. Place crepes on top of sauce, and spoon rest of marinara sauce on top of crepes. Cook in preheated 325-degree oven for 20 to 25 minutes. *Serves 4 to 5.*

After dinner Tommy totaled up Jenny's bill. We owed her $893.84, "without the sales tax." Jenny said she'd get back to us with that, seeing as she'd forgotten her calculator. Tommy threw her a grand and told her to forget about the change.

Later, after a couple of hands of pinochle, T.A. took Jenny to see Lou Rawls in the Tack Room of the Diplomat Hotel in Hallandale. When I stopped by to pick him up on the way to the track the next morning, Jenny was just leaving.

"See, Joey, she wasn't no hooker. She didn't ask for nothin' this morning. I don't pay for ____."

"You don't pay for it, Tom? What do you call free dinner, Lou Rawls, drinks all night at the Dip! Not to mention one thousand dollars worth of ____ing toothpaste?"

"*Minchia*, Joey, that ain't paying for it. That's business."

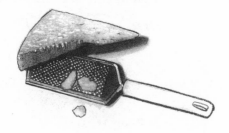

Menu

Giambotta
(Green Beans, Potato, and Tomato)

WEST PALM BEACH, FLORIDA, 1977
MY HOME

PEOPLE PRESENT:
Joe Dogs
Billy Ray (Colombo associate and hitman)

*B*illy Ray loved his wife so much he killed her. Billy was part of Little Dom's crew in New York. Stone cold. Dominick had sent him down to help me "persuade" a used-car dealer in Hollywood Beach that his health was in danger if he continued to beat up the daughter of a friend of ours. Billy Ray was a real good persuader.

Anyway, we'd just taken care of business in Hollywood (satisfactorily, I might add) and I invited Billy back to my house for dinner. My wife, Bunny, was visiting her mother for a week, and I decided to throw together a dish of giambotta. Billy followed me into the kitchen. That's when he told me how he'd whacked his wife. Hey, nothin' like a cozy chat while puttering around the kitchen, right? So Billy talked while I put together the ingredients for the giambotta.

Giambotta

4 to 5 cloves garlic, finely chopped
½ cup olive oil (extra-virgin or virgin preferred)
1 (35-ounce) can peeled tomatoes
Pinch of crushed dried oregano
2 medium to large boiling potatoes
Approximately 2 cups green beans (or sliced zucchini)
Salt and pepper to taste

A few years back, Billy began, he'd married his childhood sweetheart. Their honeymoon was interrupted when Billy had to go in for an eighteen-month stretch for assault. "When I came home," Billy continued, "I found out she was ____ing one of my so-called friends. From the first day I went into the can! I couldn't believe it. I wouldn't believe it. So I decided to test her. Told her I had to go to California on a piece of work, and that I'd be gone a week, maybe ten days. I promised to call her every night. The first night I call her from Los Angeles and tell her I love her. You know what she says to me, Joey? 'Ditto.' Ditto, Joey! Can you ____ing believe that? I knew he was there in bed with her."

I told him to save the rest of the story for dinner. I only hoped that I'd have an appetite after hearing it.

*S*lowly brown garlic in olive oil. Drain liquid from tomatoes and chop them coarsely. Add tomatoes to browned garlic and oil and cook for 20 to 30 minutes over moderate heat, stirring occasionally. Add oregano. While this is cooking, parboil potatoes and beans separately. Cook beans until tender (or *al dente* if preferred), drain, and add to tomato mixture. Cut potatoes into 1-inch cubes, add to tomato sauce, and cook for another 5 to 10 minutes. Salt and pepper to taste. Giambotta can be served as a salad or an entrée. *Serves 2.*

As we sat to eat, Billy continued his weird "love story." He said that after he hung up with his wife he picked up a hooker and banged her for $200. The next day he made arrangements with the hooker to stay in his hotel room and, for another $500, to play a role in what he told her was a practical joke. Billy gave the hooker his home telephone number and asked her to call his house—collect from Billy—at midnight eastern time. Then he hopped a flight back to New York under a *fugazy* name and picked up a hot .45 with a silencer.

The giambotta was delicious, and Billy was talking with his mouth full. "I got to my house at about 11:20 p.m., parked a block away, and opened the front door with my key. I heard a bunch of rumbling around in the bedroom. I walked in, flipped the light switch, and there they were, trying to get dressed. I shot him twice in the head and once in the heart.

"She was so scared she couldn't speak. Believe me, Joey, I didn't want to kill her. I loved her so much. If she would have ____ed around with some stranger, I'd probably still be with her. But my close friend! I let her have the other three bullets in the head. Then I turned off all the lights and poured myself a drink. At midnight the phone rang. The operator said, 'Collect call to anyone from Billy,' and I accepted.

"I disguised my voice like a broad's for a few minutes, hung up, turned on the lights, put the television on loud, and flew back to California that night.

"Joe, I had the perfect alibi. They checked it out with the airlines, the hotel, the phone company. Everyone that knows me knows that I did it. Even the law knows. But go ahead, prove it. They can't. Joe, if it happened to you, I know you'd do the same. I had to do it to save face."

I poured this maniac another glass of wine and just kept my mouth shut.

Menu

Pasta Fagioli Appetizer Soup
Veal Osso Buco

MIAMI BEACH, FLORIDA, 1977
JOHNNY IRISH'S APARTMENT

PEOPLE PRESENT:
Joe Dogs
Dominick "Little Dom" Cataldo
Johnny "Johnny Irish" Mattera (Colombo soldier)
Tony Black (Colombo soldier)
Marcia and Lu Anne (hookers)

$\mathcal{I}$t was a celebration. Johnny Irish, a hitter in the Colombo *famiglia*, had just gotten his button. He'd been made, indoctrinated, accepted as an official soldier, which is all that any of us ever wanted out of life. Little Dom was down from New York to congratulate him. He'd landed in Palm Beach, picked me up, and driven me to Johnny's apartment in Miami. Johnny's *compare*, Tony Black, was also there. There were a couple of South Beach hookers at Johnny's place. One of them was named Marcia, and I immediately fell in love. So after examining Marcia in the back bedroom, I decided to show off my culinary skills by whipping up an Italian feast fit for a newly made man.

Pasta Fagioli Appetizer Soup

3 tablespoons olive oil (extra-virgin or virgin preferred)
3 slices bacon, cut into ½-inch pieces
3 or 4 cloves garlic, crushed and chopped fine
1 (16-ounce) can small white beans (Great Northern)
1 (8-ounce) can tomato sauce plus 1½ cans water
Salt and black pepper to taste
1 basil leaf
½ pound elbow macaroni, cooked and drained
1 cup freshly grated Parmesan cheese

$\mathcal{H}$eat olive oil in medium saucepan and slowly sauté bacon and garlic until slightly browned. Add beans and sauté for 10 minutes, stirring occasionally. Add rest of ingredients except Parmesan cheese and simmer for 20 minutes. Mix cooked pasta into sauce. Discard basil leaf and serve while hot and soupy. Sprinkle Parmesan cheese over top after serving. *Serves 6.*

⌘

Veal Osso Buco

1 cup flour

Salt and pepper to taste

8 cross-cut veal shanks, 1½ inches thick

2 tablespoons corn oil

1 large white onion, chopped

4 cloves garlic, sliced paper-thin with single-edge
    razor blade

1 cup dry white wine

1 (28-ounce) can peeled tomatoes (Progresso Pomodori
    Pelati con Basilico preferred), drained and chopped

3 tablespoons tomato paste

¾ cup canned brown gravy

1 teaspoon crushed dried oregano

2 bay leaves, chopped

¼ teaspoon dried thyme

1 teaspoon Worcestershire sauce

½ teaspoon Tabasco sauce

1 teaspoon Accent (optional)

ix flour with salt and pepper and dredge veal shanks in flour, shaking off excess. Heat corn oil in large frying pan. Sauté veal on both sides, approximately 4 to 5 minutes for each side, seasoning it as you turn it. Add onion and garlic and cook for another 3 to 4 minutes. Add wine and cook over a high flame for 3 to 4 minutes to burn alcohol off. Add tomatoes, tomato paste, and brown gravy. Stir and allow to boil. Add remaining ingredients. Place entire concoction in dutch oven or casserole dish, cover, and bake in preheated 350-degree oven for 2 hours 20 minutes. Remove veal shanks from mixture and cook sauce over high heat for 2 to 3 minutes. Pour sauce over veal shanks and serve. *Serves 4.*

After dinner my heart broke when Marcia went into the back bedroom with the man of the hour, Johnny Irish. But twenty minutes later, they were back in the dining room finishing their coffee. "Johnny must be like Superman in bed," I said to Tony Black. "Faster than a speeding bullet." Tony just smiled.

Savory Stuffed Artichokes Sicilian-Style, Breaded Sautéed Steak and Greens, Zabaglione

WEST PALM BEACH, FLORIDA, 1974
MY HOUSE

PEOPLE PRESENT:

Joe Dogs	Bunny (Joe Dogs' wife)
Tommy Agro	Sandi (T.A.'s girlfriend)

*T*his one's an oldie but goodie, and worth telling you about because it kind of says it all about the Mafia. I'd only been in Florida a year or two when a friend of mine named Louie Esposito introduced me to Tommy Agro, who was to become my mentor, my rabbi, my *compare*. T.A. was a squat, florid little man, standing five-foot-three on the tip of his toes. On this tiny frame he balanced a set of incongruously large shoulders, with a belly to match. He had a headful of straight black hair, combed back neatly, that must have looked beautiful on the horse it came off of. And though he wore elevator shoes to bring him closer to the sky, he was, still, always the last one to know it was raining.

I'd known T.A. about a month, and there was just something about him that made me want to be just like him. So one night I asked him over for dinner. It was me, Bunny, T.A., and one of his Florida girls, named Sandi, a black broad with the biggest set of knockers in the universe. Tommy liked knockers almost as much as he liked exotic broads. I rarely saw him with a white woman. It was always blacks, Asians, and even an Indian once or twice.

Anyway, I really knocked myself out trying to impress him. And I think my cooking on this night was really what smoothed my way into the Gambino crime family. We started with a delicious artichoke appetizer.

Savory Stuffed Artichokes Sicilian-Style

⅓ cup plus 4 teaspoons olive oil (extra-virgin or virgin
    preferred)
1 cup finely chopped onion
1 cup chopped fresh parsley
1 cup thinly sliced celery
1 large clove garlic, chopped fine
2 ½ cups coarse fresh bread crumbs
½ cup freshly grated Parmesan cheese
⅛ teaspoon pepper
Salt to taste
½ teaspoon crushed dried oregano
2 tablespoons freshly grated Romano cheese
4 medium artichokes

Heat ⅓ cup of the oil in 10-inch frying pan. Add onion, parsley, celery, and garlic. Cook 5 to 7 minutes (until celery is almost tender). Remove from heat and stir in bread crumbs, Parmesan, pepper, salt, oregano, and Romano. Take each artichoke and cut off stem, leaving flat base. Wash in cold water and drain. Spread leaves, making sure there is space in center for stuffing. Divide stuffing into 4 portions. Spread leaves on one artichoke and spoon three-fourths of one portion of stuffing into space in center, leaving approximately one-fourth to spread between leaves. Repeat process with each artichoke until all the stuffing is used. Stand artichokes upright in large saucepan

containing 1 to 1½ inches of water and 1 teaspoon salt.
Drizzle 1 teaspoon olive oil over top of each artichoke.
Cover and cook for approximately 45 minutes, until tender.
To check for tenderness, gently pull one artichoke leaf away.
If leaf is removed easily, it's done. *Serves 4.*

✺

"*Marrone*, Joey, these are good," T.A. said as he wolfed down
the appetizer. I felt like a kid who's just gotten a straight-A report
card. "Now listen to me, Joey. If you know anyone who wants a
loan, you know, they pay the juice every week, you let me know.
But they have to be solid, you know what I mean? And you can
earn off the money, too."

I asked T.A. how much interest—or "juice," as he called
it—he charged.

"Joey, it's all according to how much they want and what we
can get without having problems. *Capisci?* Now, enough business. What's for dinner?"

Breaded Sautéed Steak and Greens

4 eggs
¾ cup olive oil (extra-virgin or virgin preferred)
2 tablespoons chopped garlic
Salt and pepper to taste
4 (12-ounce) strip steaks, ½ inch thick (trim excess fat)
1 cup flour
2 cups plain dry bread crumbs
Arugula, radicchio, and escarole leaves (enough to
make bed for steaks), tossed in olive oil, vinegar
(enough of both to coat greens), salt, and pepper

*B*eat eggs in mixing bowl. Add ½ cup olive oil, garlic, and dash of salt and pepper, and beat well. Dredge steaks in flour, shaking off excess. Dip steaks in, first, egg wash and then in bread crumbs. Sauté each steak on both sides in 1 tablespoon of remaining olive oil to desired doneness. Remove steaks. Placed tossed greens on individual plates and serve steaks on top to wilt greens. *Serves 4.*

"Tommy, I think I might know someone who needs a loan," I said over dinner. "A guy asked me the other day if I knew a shylock. I told him no, not here in Florida. But I could tell him about you and you take it from there. I think he wants $5,000."

"All right, Joey, now listen. If he mentions it to you again, tell him you know someone, but don't tell him who it is. Tell him it's five points a week. That's $250 juice a week. But don't tell him you know somebody. Wait until he asks you again. Believe me, Joey, he will. They all do. Now here's my home phone number in New York. Call me if he wants a loan. But you can call me anyway, to say hello, if you want."

I put Tommy's phone number in my wallet, but then took it out again and rewrote the number in code. I wanted to impress him. I wanted to be just like him. I wanted to be in the Mafia next to Tommy Agro, and I was ga-ga over the fact that I was doing something for him. T.A. had just become my idol, I thought, as Bunny cleared the table and I brought out dessert.

⌒〜⌒

Zabaglione

PER PERSON:

> *2 egg yolks*
> *2 teaspoons sugar*
> *¼ cup Marsala wine (or sherry)*
> *Fresh fruit (strawberries or raspberries preferred)*

*B*eat yolks and sugar until well blended. Stir in Marsala or sherry. Place mixture in large bowl and place over medium heat. Whisk constantly while cooking until texture is thick (being very, very careful not to curdle). Pour over fresh fruit.

After dinner Tommy and I retired to the living room while the girls did the dishes. T.A. thought it was time for a heart-to-heart.

"Joey, I want you to relax," he began. "I know you're trying to impress me, but don't knock yourself out. I'm impressed with you. I'm impressed with your wife. I like the way you handle yourself. Now here's what I want you to do. Find yourself some more customers. Expand yourself. Do things. And if you have any problems, call me. I'll help you. But, on the other hand, if you do good, don't forget me. Because I have my own *compare,* and I can't forget him.

"In this life," T.A. continued, "when you eat alone, you die alone. Remember what I'm telling you. You think you knew people before? Forget about them. You belong to an organization now that is the biggest. Joey, when you're with me, there is no one in this ____ing world that can ____ with you. Not even the Pope. But there is one thing that I noticed that is one of your biggest detriments. You bring your wife along with you all the time, wherever you go. You got to stop bringing her around so much, Joey. It just don't look good."

Orecchietti with Peas and Prosciutto

Lake Worth, Florida, 1978
Little Dom's Crash Pad

People Present:
Joe Dogs
Dominick "Little Dom" Cataldo

"*W*ake up, Joey, I'm flying in tonight." It was Dominick Cataldo's voice on the other end of the phone. "Pick me up at Lauderdale at nine-fifteen. I'm on Delta. You got to do something for me. I can't come dressed, so have some clothes for me and for you. *Capisci?*"

Little Dom was telling me he couldn't carry a gun on the plane and he wanted me to get us a couple. "What size jacket do you want me to bring?" I asked.

"I wear a thirty-eight," Dom said. "And listen, you know those slacks you got for my girl? She has a twenty-two waist. Bring them, too."

Later that night I picked up Dominick, he handed me an address in the Keys, and we drove south. I was packing two snub-nosed .38s and a little .22. Dom took one .38 and the .22 and stuffed them into his waistband.

"Dom, what the hell is coming down?"

"It's nothing, Joey. I just have to talk to some guys. I just need the pieces in case they don't hear so good. It'll only be a couple of minutes. In fact, you don't even have to turn the car off."

I found the place. Small ranch house–cum–fishing shack nestled inside a shadowy cove of bougainvillea. "Go around the block and park," Little Dom barked.

As I backed the car up, Dominick put on a long blond wig. Then he covered his face with a black beard and mustache.

"You go ahead," he said. "Drop me off on the corner, and after I go in, pull up in front of the house with the lights off and the car running. Don't ask no ____ing questions."

I didn't. I dropped him off and he minced up to the front door like a fag. I watched him enter, and once he got inside I began to pull up the car. I heard about twelve shots. Dominick came walking out and hopped into the passenger seat.

"Let's go," he said. "Take me to that safe apartment my *famiglia* keeps in Lake Worth and make me something to eat. That prosciutto thing you made last time sounds good." Who was I to argue? Here's my recipe for "that prosciutto thing."

⌒♫⌒

Orecchietti with Peas and Prosciutto

½ pound thick-cut prosciutto, diced
½ cup olive oil (extra-virgin or virgin preferred)
1 tablespoon chopped onion
1½ cups fresh or frozen peas
1 pound orecchietti
2 tablespoons butter
½ cup freshly grated Parmesan cheese

Brown diced prosciutto in olive oil in a frying pan until crisp. Remove prosciutto with slotted spoon and set aside. Add onion to oil and cook until translucent. Add peas and cooked prosciutto and allow to simmer over extremely low heat while preparing pasta. Boil orecchietti until *al dente*. Drain pasta and place in large bowl. Add butter and cheese, a little at a time, while tossing pasta. Add pea and prosciutto mixture. Toss and serve. Again, this is a rich sauce—perfect for killer appetites. Ha ha. *Serves 4.*

Over dinner Dom told me that a couple of Colombians had beaten him and his *compare,* the Colombo capo Allie LaMonte, out of $80,000 on a dope deal. "I needed the disguise in the event someone else was there," he said. "And it was a good thing, too. There was a broad and two young kids."

"Dominick! You didn't?"

"Naw, Joey, I don't hurt kids or women. But without the disguise, I wouldn't have had no choice. Christ, I was hungry. Joey, this meal is delicious."

He just whacked a couple of guys and Dom was starving! Sometimes I couldn't believe the people I was hanging around with. On the way home I drove over a bridge and dropped the pieces into the Miami River. Then I needed a drink. I stopped at the Diplomat Hotel, caught the last show in the Tack Room, met a good-looking chick, and spent the night in a suite. I always got a room at the Dip dirt cheap. They gave me convention rates.

Menu

Pot Roast à la Joe Dogs

West Palm Beach, Florida, 1969
My Apartment

People Present:
Joe Dogs
Bunny
Mike "Midge" Belvedere (Colombo associate and bookmaker)
Ann (Midge's wife)

My very first *compare* was Mike "Midge" Belvedere, a bookmaker from Long Island, New York. Midge was also connected to the Colombo crime family. Midge and his wife, Ann, were my son's godparents. Midge was a very good-looking guy, a bronze Sicilian with thick, wavy black hair and dark, dark eyes. Almost black. When he stared at you, you felt like knives were going through your head.

Midge's wife Ann was beautiful. She looked like Elizabeth Taylor but had a better body. But once she opened her mouth, *marrone*, you'd think she learned to talk at truck driver's school.

Soon after Bunny and I had moved to Florida, Midge and Ann flew south for a visit. I was still getting established, we were living in an apartment, we hadn't even bought our house yet, and money was a little tight. Not real tight, just a little. Anyway, the four of us were going out to see a late show, Sergio Franchi was playing a hotel in North Miami. But first I wanted to cook the Belvederes a great dinner.

Pot Roast à la Joe Dogs

Salt and pepper to taste
1 (3-pound) chuck roast (with bone in it)
5 carrots
5 celery stalks
1 large onion
4 Idaho potatoes (or 8 new, or red, potatoes)

1 (10 ¾-ounce) can cream of mushroom soup
   (Campbell's preferred) plus 1¼ cans water
1½ tablespoons Dijon mustard
1 tablespoon Gravy Master

*S*alt and pepper roast on both sides. Place roast in good-size pan and cook in preheated 400-degree oven for 20 minutes to brown. While meat is cooking, clean and cut carrots into 2-inch pieces. Repeat process with celery stalks. Cut onion into 8 pieces. Peel and halve potatoes. Mix mushroom soup and water in large bowl. Add mustard and Gravy Master for color and flavor. Mix well. Remove roast from oven and place vegetables around meat in pan. Pour sauce mixture over meat and vegetables, cover with aluminum foil, and bake for 2 hours at 350 degrees. Should be served with Dewar's White Label scotch on rocks. *Serves 4.*

◈

Later, as the four of us were walking out of the Sergio Franchi show, the television actress Joi Lansing pushed through the mob waiting for the valet to retrieve the cars. Now Joi Lansing was best known for her, shall we say, awesome headlights. And as she approached our group, Joi smiled at Midge and sort of gave him the eye. Ann sidled up to her real slowly and said, "If you don't take your ____in' eyes off my husband, I'll smack you in the face with your own big ____, you ____in' whore."

Ann was beautiful. And she set the tone that first night for a wonderful time.

Chicken Cacciatore
Northern-Style

HOLLYWOOD, FLORIDA, 1972
THE OLD PELICAN RESTAURANT

PEOPLE PRESENT:
Joe Dogs
Louie Esposito

*P*erfect timing.

Louie Esposito was on the lam from another big robbery attempt. Louie was a great B&E man, and he'd gotten a tip about a house in New Jersey that was home to some $2 million in cash, stashed in some fake books in the library. Louie and a partner had dressed up as priests, faked a flat tire, and chloroformed the maid who let them into the house.

"We saw the ____ing money, Joey," he told me. "Stacked up in these empty books. A ____ load. But we musta tripped a wire. Within two minutes there were sirens and squad cars all over the place."

Empty-handed, Louie and the other guy ran into some woods behind the house and split up, and Louie spent the night in the rafters of an empty construction site. The cops caught his partner. Louie told me he was on the lam because he didn't know if the guy had given him up.

Coincidentally, not two nights before, me and my crew had busted up a joint, the Old Pelican Restaurant, on orders from Tommy Agro. The two brothers who owned the place were late with their vig. We hadn't torched the building, but it was closed. We'd really done a job—with sledgehammers and axes—on the bar and the dining room. But the kitchen was still intact. And there was an office with a cot.

Tommy Varaggo, one of the owners, had flown to New York for a sitdown with T.A. His brother Jimmy knew better than to come near the place. So I took Louie—who hadn't been present at the bashing two nights before—to the restaurant, tossed him the key, and told him to make himself at home. Then I cooked him dinner.

Chicken Cacciatore
Northern-Style

2 to 3 tablespoons olive oil (extra-virgin or virgin preferred)
1 (2½-pound) chicken, cut into pieces
1 large onion, chopped into ¼-inch pieces
3 cloves garlic, crushed and chopped fine
2 shallots, chopped fine
½ cup dry white wine
1½ teaspoons red wine vinegar
Salt and pepper to taste
2 basil leaves (dried or fresh)

*H*eat olive oil in large frying pan. Sauté chicken over medium heat, turning occasionally, for approximately 20 minutes. While chicken browns, add onion, garlic, and shallots to pan. After 20 minutes or so, add wine, vinegar, salt, pepper, and basil to mixture. Cover tightly, and allow to simmer for another 30 minutes. Serve with pasta, rice, or vegetable. *Serves 4.*

Over dinner, something stuck in my craw (and not the chicken, which was delicious). Louie said he was on the lam from the Jersey robbery. Yet less than a year earlier his cut from the big Aqueduct Racetrack heist had come to close to a million bucks. When I asked him what happened to all that dough, a queer look kind of crossed his face.

"Are you kidding, Joey?" he asked. "My share was only $800,000. I went through that in a couple of months. Gee, though, I just wish I coulda paid off my house. Anyway, I have to find some work until I make another score. You got a job for me?"

Nobody in our organization could ever hold on to a buck. We all threw money around. Broads and more broads. Lawyers for pinches, bondsmen for bail. The lawyers got the most, though. We called them whores. They got that name from jumping from one client to another. I had a good lawyer. I got sentenced to a month one time. He got me out in thirty days.

Menu

Spinach and Eggplant Lasagna with Sun-Dried Tomato Sauce
Peach Cobbler

HOLLYWOOD, FLORIDA, 1980
NENA'S APARTMENT

PEOPLE PRESENT:
Joe Dogs   Tommy Agro
Popo Tortora (Genovese soldier and dope dealer)
Frank Dean (Genovese associate and Tortora's muscle)

*J*t was our version of going to the mattresses. Popo Tortora was a big doper with the Genovese family in south Florida, and he was at war with us. The problem was Popo's, though. He'd sold me some bad blow—six keys of coke—and I'd refused to pay. The crap wasn't fit to stuff up your ____, much less your nose, and I'd told Popo so. But he was making innuendoes like I'd switched his dope on him. Naturally, shots were fired. But nobody'd been hit. Yet.

The situation got so bad, however, that Tommy Agro had flown down from New York with some muscle after I got word that Popo was going to make a run at me at one of my hangouts, a restaurant owned by a friend of mine.

Anyway, six of us—all Gambinos—sat up all night at this restaurant, armed to the ____ing teeth, waiting for an attack that never came. Finally, one of Tommy's sluggers went hunting on his own and capped one of Popo's crew after a bar fight. That was enough for the big boys up in New York. This they didn't need. The Feds were coming down on us hard enough as it was, and they didn't want us fighting among ourselves and attracting attention. So T.A.'s *compare,* the Gambino family *consigliere* Joe N. Gallo (not to be confused with Crazy Joey Gallo of the Colombos), ordered a sitdown.

We scheduled the meet at my girlfriend Nena's apartment in Hollywood. By this time my wife, Bunny, had tossed me out of the house for cheatin' like a jackrabbit. I was living with Nena, a real babydoll and a flight attendant for American Airlines with a body to die for. Luckily, she was on a West Coast turnaround when the meet went down.

Popo brought one of his top sluggers, a nasty piece of business named Frank Dean. T.A. and I ushered them in and frisked them. We'd laid our guns out on the living room couch, and expected them to do the same. Tommy had just been diagnosed with a heart condition, and didn't want any meat. So I went instead with a delicious, and meatless, lasagna. See how I looked after my *compare?* See what a nice guy I was? *Minchia,* if I had known how Tommy was gonna eventually look after me, I woulda shoved a twenty-ounce porterhouse down his throat. But I digress. Here's the recipe for the tomato sauce.

Spinach and Eggplant Lasagna with Sun-Dried Tomato Sauce

TOMATO SAUCE

> *8 cups chopped fresh plum tomatoes*
> *½ cup sun-dried tomatoes (soaked in 1 cup water)*
> *1 red pepper, seeded and quartered*
> *1 onion, peeled and chopped*
> *1 clove garlic, crushed and chopped fine*
> *2 cups vegetable broth (or water)*
> *½ teaspoon salt (or to taste)*
> *½ teaspoon black pepper (or to taste)*
> *½ cup fresh basil leaves, chopped*

*C*ombine plum tomatoes, sun-dried tomatoes (and their liquid), red pepper, onion, garlic, and broth in saucepan. Allow to simmer, uncovered, for 45 minutes. Add salt and pepper to taste. As sauce is simmering—say, every 15 minutes or so—add basil leaves until all are used. *Makes 6 cups sauce.*

The sitdown wasn't as harrowing as I thought it would be. Granted, Frank Dean had a face and an attitude that could stop a train. But Popo was all smiles and backslaps. Popo was a scrawny old man, in his mid-sixties, and aside from dope he had a nice business going in forged airline tickets. He had someone inside at the airlines, and he could get you any ticket you wanted, on any carrier, at half price. As I was running back and forth between the kitchen and the living room he must have offered me free tickets ten times. I also heard him telling Tommy that he was sure our "little squabble" could be solved amicably, and after it was, he was going to call over the most gorgeous hookers either of us had ever seen. Now, because of his doping, Popo always had broads galore. And I liked a good hooker as much as the next guy. But this wasn't a good sign. If there was one thing I'd learned by now about T.A., it was that his little head always did all his thinking for his big head. And I didn't need his little head getting in the way of any negotiations. This was as good a time as any to put together the lasagna.

5 medium eggplants, cut into ⅜-inch rounds
2 to 3 teaspoons salt
2 teaspoons fresh thyme (or ½ to 1 teaspoon dried)
1 bunch spinach, stemmed, washed, and lightly steamed
4 cups low-fat ricotta cheese (Polly-O brand preferred)
2 cups chopped fresh basil leaves
1 egg
1 teaspoon black pepper
Tomato Sauce (recipe above)
12 dry lasagna noodles (or pre-boiled, if preferred)
1 (8-ounce) package mozzarella cheese, thinly sliced
    (optional)

Sprinkle eggplant with 2 to 3 teaspoons salt (depending on taste and heart condition). Set aside in colander to drain for 30 minutes. Rinse and pat eggplant dry. Combine eggplant and thyme in nonstick frying pan over medium to low heat. Cook, a few at a time, on both sides until barely tender. Place in bowl and set aside. Also set aside lightly steamed spinach. Combine ricotta, basil leaves, egg, and salt and pepper to taste and set aside. Spread 2 cups of tomato sauce along bottom of 9- by 9-inch baking dish. Place 4 uncooked lasagna noodles over sauce. (*Note:* Pre-boil if pasta is preferred well done, as noodles will be *al dente* if cooked dry in recipe.) Top with a third each of spinach, ricotta mixture, and eggplant and 1 cup sauce. Repeat procedure twice, ending with a layer of sauce. Add top layer of thinly sliced mozzarella (optional). Cover with foil and

bake in preheated 350-degree oven for 45 minutes. Remove foil and bake an additional 15 to 20 minutes.

During dinner Tommy started bragging to Popo about how healthy he'd been eating. "How do I look, Popo?" he'd ask. "Don't I look thinner?" Popo, who wasn't much interested, nodded his assent. Then, after we were done, Tommy said—in all seriousness—"Well, I may be thinner, but I feel like I'm eating like a ____ing rabbit. Joey, you got any bacon and eggs and toast back there? I need some meat." About this time I was wishing he'd die of a heart attack right there.

As it was, we straightened out the dope dispute over dessert, a tasty peach cobbler I'd thrown together especially for the occasion. Popo agreed to call a truce if we could help him lay off the bum dope. T.A. knew a couple of knockaround Lucchese guys who sold to college kids—college kids never know good dope—and agreed to contact them. The hookers showed in time for coffee and the cobbler. Sweets for the sweet, right? A week later all was back to normal.

Peach Cobbler

6 to 8 fresh peaches, peeled
Confectioners' sugar and cinnamon to taste
1 cup flour
½ teaspoon baking powder
⅛ teaspoon salt
½ pound (2 sticks) butter, softened
1 cup granulated sugar
1 egg, beaten
½ teaspoon vanilla

*M*ix peaches with desired amount of confectioners' sugar and cinnamon in bottom of 9- by 13-inch baking pan. Mix together flour, baking powder, and salt. Cream together softened butter and granulated sugar and add to flour mixture. Fold in egg and vanilla. Spread cobbler mixture over fruit and bake in preheated 375-degree oven for 35 to 40 minutes. Dust with additional confectioners' sugar and serve with ice cream while cobbler is still warm.

P.S.: Two years later the Feds issued a narcotics-trafficking indictment on Popo Tortora. They came to arrest him at his hotel in Miami. He was sunning himself at the pool. When he saw the G approaching, his heart seized up and he died right there in his lounge chair. We should all be so lucky.

Menu

Fish en Papillote
in Béchamel Sauce

NORTH MIAMI BEACH, FLORIDA, 1980
JIGGS FORLANO'S APARTMENT

PEOPLE PRESENT:
Joe Dogs
Jiggs Forlano

*T*heir big mistake was trying to scam a scammer. To make a long story short, I was still living with Nena when Bunny called to say our house had been robbed. It turned out it was just some neighborhood kids, but I took the insurance company for all I could get, including a claim that my wife's $10,000 diamond ring had been stolen. Of course, I had hidden the ring real good before I claimed it was missing.

At any rate, the insurance company made good, and I picked up a replacement ring from a Miami jeweler. But a few months later, when I went to hock the piece, my pal Jiggs—the "retired" Colombo capo and a jewelry expert—informed me that it was costume. I hit the roof. Jiggs agreed to accompany me to the jewelry store, because he knew the people who ran it.

Jiggs and I walked into the jeweler's separately, with Jiggs walking to a corner, pretending to be window shopping. He was carrying a small fishing gaff under his coat. He told me that if anyone gave me a problem he'd be more than happy to rip their eyes out. I walked to the counter and signaled to the guy who had originally sold me the stone. I'd called before, so they knew I was coming.

"Here's your piece of glass, you crooked ____," I said.

"Don't talk to me that way," this guy says. "Who do you think you are? I'm giving you $6,000 for that ring, and no more."

With that, I reached over, grabbed this moron by the tie, and backhanded him. Then I pulled his head down onto the jewelry case, cracking the thick glass. He started bleeding from the nose and mouth. Just then, Jiggs appeared at my side. "Hi, Joe," he said, smiling amiably and flashing the gaff. "You got a problem here, or what?"

"No, Jiggs, I don't think so. My friend here has a nosebleed, and I'm trying to tell him what's good for it."

The clerk recognized Jiggs, nodded hello, ran back to his office, and came back with a $10,000 check. He'd left the name blank.

I said, "Listen, get one of your flunkies to cash this check right away. I want cash, *capisci?*"

He went back to his office, returned with the cash, and ordered a salesgirl to bring me a solid-gold bracelet. "Keep it, with our compliments." Later, I mailed Tommy Agro $2,000 and the bracelet. When I earned, T.A. earned.

On the drive back to Jiggs' place in North Miami I slipped the old capo a grand for his trouble. Then I made him dinner, his favorite, Fish en Papillote in Béchamel Sauce.

Fish en Papillote in Béchamel Sauce

BÉCHAMEL SAUCE

> *5 tablespoons butter*
> *5 tablespoons flour*
> *4 cups hot milk*
> *Salt and pepper to taste*
> *Pinch of grated nutmeg*

Melt butter in saucepan. When hot, add flour and stir for approximately 2 minutes. (Important: Do not scorch!) Pour in 1½ cups of milk and stir with whisk over low heat. As mixture comes to boil, slowly add rest of milk and the salt, pepper, and nutmeg. Cook for approximately 15 minutes over low heat, stirring occasionally.

FISH

> 2 pompano fillets (can also use red snapper)
> Salt and pepper to taste
> Papillote bag (purchase in specialty supermarket)
> 1 teaspoon chopped shallot
> 1 tablespoon chopped celery
> 3 tablespoons Béchamel Sauce (recipe above)

Season your fish with salt and pepper and place fillets in bag. Add all other ingredients and tie bag tightly with accompanying tie. Bake in preheated 350-degree oven for 20 minutes. The bag will rise but will not tear. When serving, pierce bag with knife and pour onto plate (or over rice) with all the juices. *Serves 2.*

Menu

Baked Chicken à la Joe Dogs

LAKE GEORGE, NEW YORK, 1980
THE HOLIDAY INN

PEOPLE PRESENT:
Joe Dogs
Brooke (Joe's girlfriend)
Dominick "Little Dom" Cataldo
Lorraine (Little Dom's girlfriend)

$\mathcal{I}$'d been a member of Tommy Agro's Gambino crew for over ten years now. In spite of T.A.'s warnings, I was double-banging him behind his back. It just didn't seem right that I could only earn from one *famiglia*. It was undemocratic. So when Little Dom called from New York and wanted to know if I could score him some pot, I didn't think twice about doing business with the Colombos. The Gambinos always looked down on the Colombos anyway, like they were junior members of the mob. And it's a fact that they did a lot of the Gambinos' dirty work. Most Colombos were crazy. So I felt like I was working with distant relatives, though I know Tommy wouldn't have seen it that way.

Anyway, I scored 580 pounds of Colombian Gold for $130 a pound and sent it north to Little Dom with Billy Ray on the autotrain, and three weeks later Dom called to say he'd offered the entire consignment to one guy at $285 a pound. We made $45,000 apiece, which called for a celebration. Dom suggested I grab a broad and meet him in Lake George, beautiful country in the summertime.

I flew up the next day with a cute little honey I'd just met named Brooke and met Dom in his luxury suite. He was there with his girlfriend Lorraine. I hadn't seen Dom in a while, and it was a happy reunion. The night was so beautiful, the air so sweet, that I didn't feel like fixing any heavy Italian food. We settled on baked chicken, the perfect summertime dish.

Baked Chicken à la Joe Dogs

4 chicken breasts (remove skin but leave bones in)
1 tablespoon pepper
2 or 3 (to taste) cloves garlic, crushed and chopped
2 teaspoons crushed dried oregano
4 new (red) potatoes cut into ¼-inch rounds (leave skin on)
2 small onions, quartered
1 tablespoon garlic salt
1 tablespoon Accent (optional)
2 cups chicken stock
1 (15-ounce) can sweet peas

*P*lace chicken breasts, facing bone down, in 14- by 10-inch baking pan or dish. Sprinkle pepper, chopped garlic cloves, and oregano over meaty tops. Arrange potatoes and onions in pan around chicken. Sprinkle garlic salt and Accent (optional) over top of everything and pour 1 cup of chicken stock over chicken breasts. Cover pan or dish and cook in preheated 350-degree oven for 45 minutes. After 45 minutes, remove cover and pour the other cup of chicken stock, as well as can of sweet peas, including juice, over concoction. Bake, uncovered, for another 20 to 25 minutes. Serve with rice and Dewar's White Label scotch. *Serves 4.*

After dinner Brooke raised her eyebrows when Dom pulled out a peanut butter jar filled with cocaine. He began drawing lines on the glass table and handed me a straw. He knew I didn't do that stuff, but I guess he was testing me. I declined. So he snorted some and Lorraine snorted some, but Brooke was hesitant. So to put her at ease I snorted a line, but Brooke still refused.

We went to the lounge for a few drinks, but after taking that snort I began to feel nauseated. I excused myself and went to the men's room to upchuck. When I returned the girls were gone. Dom said they'd been in the ladies' room for quite a while. "I bet Lorraine turns Brooke on," he added. I didn't care one way or the other. It was her nose and her business. But Little Dom was right, because when the girls came back Brooke was talking a mile a minute.

During one of the girls' many subsequent trips to the ladies' room, Dom leaned across the table and told me a secret. "My friend Johnny Irish has a big problem," he said. "He led the FBI from Florida to where the boss was on Long Island." Dom was referring to Carmine "the Snake" Persico. "Now the Snake is really pissed off."

I was stunned. Dom was telling me that Johnny Irish was probably not long for this world. I told Dom I didn't want to know any more, and he didn't bring it up for the rest of the evening.

But that night, driving back to our hotel room with Brooke, Johnny Irish was all I could think about. In our business, they'd turn on you and have you capped in a minute. Did this mean that Little Dom or Tommy Agro, my two best friends in the world, could someday turn on me? Brooke talked like a jackrabbit all the way back to our room. That's not all she did like a jackrabbit that night. And I was surprised. Brooke was a natural blonde.

Menu

Mussels in Light Sauce

QUEENS, NEW YORK, 1980
LITTLE DOM CATALDO'S APARTMENT

PEOPLE PRESENT:
Joe Dogs
Dominick "Little Dom" Cataldo
Carol (Little Dom's girlfriend)

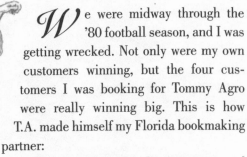

*W*e were midway through the '80 football season, and I was getting wrecked. Not only were my own customers winning, but the four customers I was booking for Tommy Agro were really winning big. This is how T.A. made himself my Florida bookmaking partner:

"Joey, let these guys bet into you, and you keep the tabs. We'll split the winnings. But if they win, I'm out. I'm not your partner no more."

So it went, "belonging" to Tommy Agro.

So I got shafted. What's new? October. November. December. I took a major bath. I was tapped. And not only was I losing in football, I was also getting killed at the track. So it was a godsend when Little Dom called from New York and told me he'd gotten rid of some coke I'd shipped him during the past summer. My end came to 150 large, and I told Dom I'd be on the next flight to New York to collect.

That night, Little Dom and I were divvying up the cash in his girlfriend's apartment in Queens when he told me to make a shopping list for dinner. I was in the mood for mussels, and Dom sent the broad out to pick up the food. By the way, those ten pounds of mussels are no mistake—these are guys with hearty appetites. And that goes for some of the broads, too.

Mussels in Light Sauce

10 pounds fresh mussels, scrubbed clean
4 cloves garlic, smashed
¼ pound (1 stick) butter
4 dried chili peppers, crushed
¼ cup chopped fresh parsley
Juice of 1 lemon
¼ teaspoon pepper
1 cup dry white wine
2 tablespoons cooking sherry
1 cup peeled tomatoes, drained and chopped
4 tablespoons chopped fresh parsley
½ teaspoon dried crushed oregano
8 chopped fresh bay leaves or crumbled dried bay leaves

Place mussels in a big pot, add 2 garlic cloves, ½ stick butter, chilies, parsley, lemon juice, pepper, and water ½ inch above mussels. Cover and bring to boil. Remove mussels when shells open, which should take about 15 minutes. Pour juice from mussels into a frying pan and set mussels aside. Melt remaining ½ stick butter in pan containing mussel juice. In pan, sauté remaining garlic for approximately 1½ to 2½ minutes, or until limp. Add wine and sherry and cook for another 3 minutes over high heat. Add chopped tomatoes, parsley, oregano, and bay leaves and cook for 12 minutes over medium to high heat, stirring several times. Place mussels, still in shell, on baking tray. Pour tomato mixture over mussels and bake in preheated 400-degree oven for 4 additional minutes. Serve with garlic bread and pasta. *Serves 3 or 4.*

After our delicious feast, Dom walked me out to his car and told me I had to do him a favor. "Let's take a ride," he said.

"Sure, Dom. What is it?"

"I have to go up the Taconic Parkway and dig a hole," he told me. "I got this mother_____ in the car and I need a hand getting him into the hole. I'll do the digging. I just need a hand getting him out of the trunk. I just can't leave him in the streets, Joey. This guy was a made man with the Lucchese family."

He had to be kidding. I began backing away from his car. "Dom, you're not serious, right? You don't really have a _____ing body in the trunk, do you?"

"Hey, Joe, what the _____'s wrong with you?" he said. "Why would I tell you a story like that?"

With that, he popped the trunk. There was a body inside, all right, all twisted up. The hole in this poor sap's forehead had already formed a bloody scab. I felt sick. I wished I hadn't cooked mussels. I had to get out of there.

"Joey, this guy's been in my trunk for three days now, and he's starting to stink. I need a hand. What do you say?"

"Dominick, I'm going to tell you like T.A. would say it. I wasn't made with a finger. What do you want to do, make another two-story job? _____ you! Get someone else to help you. I don't want to know where your burial grounds are."

"Yeah, Joey, I guess I can't blame you," he finally said after a long, icy moment. "But that's not what I had in mind, honest. Not to worry, I'll get someone else to help."

"Yeah," I said, "and make sure it's somebody you don't like." And with that, we hopped a cab to the nearest bar.

Menu

Just Desserts

WEST PALM BEACH, FLORIDA, MARCH 1981

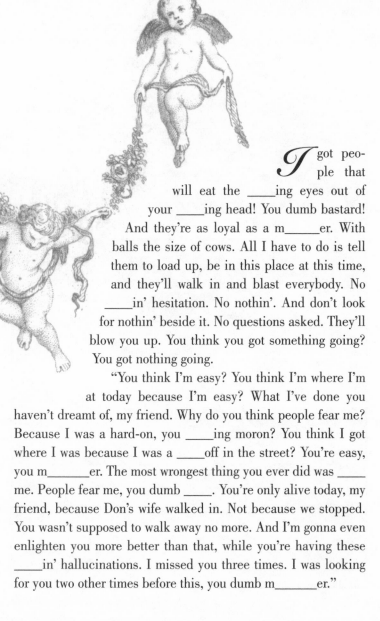

I got people that will eat the ____ing eyes out of your ____ing head! You dumb bastard! And they're as loyal as a m____er. With balls the size of cows. All I have to do is tell them to load up, be in this place at this time, and they'll walk in and blast everybody. No ____in' hesitation. No nothin'. And don't look for nothin' beside it. No questions asked. They'll blow you up. You think you got something going? You got nothing going.

"You think I'm easy? You think I'm where I'm at today because I'm easy? What I've done you haven't dreamt of, my friend. Why do you think people fear me? Because I was a hard-on, you ____ing moron? You think I got where I was because I was a ____off in the street? You're easy, you m____er. The most wrongest thing you ever did was ____ me. People fear me, you dumb ____. You're only alive today, my friend, because Don's wife walked in. Not because we stopped. You wasn't supposed to walk away no more. And I'm gonna even enlighten you more better than that, while you're having these ____in' hallucinations. I missed you three times. I was looking for you two other times before this, you dumb m____er."

That was the apoplectic Tommy Agro, calling me from New York. You might say we'd had a falling-out. I lay in my bed, holding the telephone receiver at arm's length, listening to T.A. screaming at the top of his lungs. My head ached. My broken ribs burned like kindling. And my nose, splayed across my face, was split down the middle. To T.A.'s dismay, I was still alive. Barely.

Six weeks earlier, Tommy A. and two of his sluggers had flown south with the intention of beating me to death. They'd used a baseball bat and a lead pipe, and the last thing I remember before losing consciousness was Tommy digging his dainty little alligator loafer into my ribs. And all because I was a lousy three months late on my vig! I'd only survived through fate. Just as T.A. was about to chop off my right hand with a meat cleaver—Mafia symbolism—Don Ritz's wife had walked into the kitchen of Don Ritz's Pizzeria on Singer Island, where the beating had taken place, and let out a bloodcurdling scream. She'd spooked the sluggers, and they'd fled.

I'd awakened three days later in St. Mary's Hospital. The priest giving me last rites called it a miracle. My mother and daughters were there in the hospital room. As well as my wife and my girlfriend. And FBI agents Larry Doss and Gunnar Askland.

Now, six weeks later, Tommy was letting me know he hadn't cooled down. I sipped my scotch, smiled, and watched the tape recorder attached to the telephone unspool. The tape recorder was courtesy of the Florida FBI. But the revenge was going to be all mine. The Feds had dubbed our gig "Operation Home Run," because of the way they'd used my head for batting practice. They should have called it "Operation Tunnel Vision," because I was going underground with one thing in mind. Getting even.

Menu

Steak au Poivre

Lake Worth, Florida, 1981
My New Apartment

People Present:
Joe Dogs
Tony Amoroso (FBI supervising agent)
Larry Doss (FBI agent)
Gunnar Askland (FBI agent)
Rossi (FBI agent)

*J*oey, we're bringing in a new agent to go undercover with you," said Case Agent Larry Doss. "That's what Tony wants. And he wants you to pick the agent you feel most comfortable with. Tony's bringing over someone tonight for you to meet. So what are you cooking for dinner?"

I was sitting in my new apartment in the backass end of Lake Worth, far from the madding crowd and far from the Mafia, which two months earlier had tried to kill me. With me were FBI agents Larry Doss and Gunnar Askland, my case agent and his assistant. The Eye was paying for this apartment and everything in it, including me. I was now working for the Feds, with one thing on my mind. Revenge. I wanted to see Tommy Agro buried.

Doss and Askland's supervisor, Special Agent Tony Amoroso, was on his way over. I had convinced Tony that if he could just get me straight, monetarily, with T.A., I could worm my way back into the mob's good graces. I'd wear a wire. I'd tap telephone calls. I'd do anything to nail T.A.'s ass. Amoroso agreed, on the condition that I work with some backup. Tonight, he was bringing a potential undercover over for dinner. I was making Steak au Poivre, for five. The key is how you make the veal stock, which you have to do a day ahead of time.

Steak au Poivre

Veal Stock

> ¼ cup olive oil (extra-virgin or virgin preferred)
> 2 or 3 veal bones (butcher will cut for you)
> 1 gallon water (enough to cover bones in pot)
> 4 celery tops
> 6 to 10 tomato ends
> 2 onions
> 2 carrots
> 2 tablespoons tomato paste

*H*eat olive oil in 8-quart stockpot and brown bones. When browned, add just enough water to cover bones and throw in vegetables. Bring to a boil and allow to simmer, uncovered, for anywhere from 12 to 24 hours (24 preferred). As water evaporates, replace. Two hours from finish, add tomato paste. Now allow water to evaporate. When you get to about half the liquid you started with, it's done. Strain and freeze in 1-cup portions for later use.

Supervising Agent Tony Amoroso showed up with the undercover agent as I was setting the table. He had to be joking! The guy Amoroso brought in, an agent named Rossi, was Italian all right. But he looked to be about sixteen years old. *Marrone.*

STEAK

> 3 tablespoons olive oil (extra-virgin or virgin preferred)
> ½ cup crushed peppercorns
> 5 (8- to 10-ounce) filets mignons
> 1 cup Veal Stock (recipe above)
> 2 ounces cognac (Rémy Martin preferred)
> 3 tablespoons heavy cream
> Salt and black pepper to taste

*W*hile olive oil heats in large frying pan, press peppercorns into both sides of steaks. Cook steaks in olive oil to your desired doneness (rare preferred). Remove steaks and place in 150-degree oven to keep warm. Add stock and cognac to olive oil and meat drippings in pan. Step back and ignite. After flame burns out pour heavy cream into mixture and cook over medium heat for roughly 5 minutes until mixture is reduced by half or less, stirring repeatedly. Season with salt and pepper while stirring. Spoon some sauce onto each plate. Place steaks on top of sauce and spoon remaining sauce over top of steaks.

Agent Rossi was professional, and he was anxious, and as we wolfed down our steaks I gave him the lay of the land. "These aren't just kids or bank robbers we're dealing with here," I explained. "They're hardened criminals and killers. If you think for one minute that if they find out you're an FBI agent you're safe, forget it. They'll chop you up and then grind up the parts so no one will ever find you. They'll flush you down the toilet and your friends here will be burying an empty casket."

Then I played for Agent Rossi Tommy Agro's infamous "eat the ____ing eyes out of your ____ing head" tape.

"What's wrong, Agent Rossi? Don't you like my steak? You look a little pale. You want to lie down?"

Agent Rossi didn't pass the screen test. He'd never be able to hack it. He knew it. We knew it. No hard feelings.

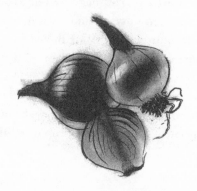

Menu

Shrimp Scampi Gambino-Style

HALLANDALE, FLORIDA, 1982
POOLSIDE AT THE DIPLOMAT HOTEL

PEOPLE PRESENT:
Joe Dogs
Tommy Agro
Checko Brown (Colombo soldier)
Anthony "Fat Andy" Ruggiano (Gambino capo)
Skinny Bobby DeSimone
Paulie Principe and Frank Russo (Gambino associates and sluggers)

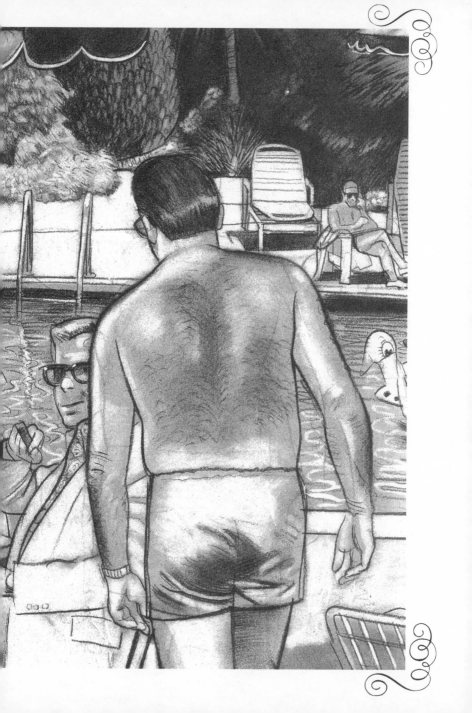

*T*ommy Agro called at midnight.

I was now in the habit of pressing the "record" button whenever I picked up the phone. I always made sure there was a fresh tape in the machine. The only person I didn't tape, I wouldn't tape, was Little Dom. It was part of the deal.

"I'm here, Joey, at the Dip. Come and see me tomorrow."

"I'm hurt, T.A.," I whimpered. "I'm hurt bad. Please don't hurt me anymore. I didn't do anything wrong. Can't it be over? Can't we start fresh?"

My begging was not a facade. I was really afraid. I hadn't seen Tommy since the beating—five weeks ago—and I dreaded facing him so soon. My head was still a mess. The scars from the stitches were still raw.

"Joey, I'm not gonna do nothin' to you," he said. "I'm down here for somethin' else. Believe me, it's all over. I'll never do that again."

On the drive down I–95 that morning I watched the Feds tailing me through my rearview mirror. I'd wanted to wear a wire, but they'd forbidden it. Said it was too dangerous so soon. The valet at the Dip barely recognized me, my head was so swollen. The Olympic-size pool was packed with tourists. Tommy's cabana, complete with kitchen, was at the south end, near the wading pool. My stomach sank when the first guys I saw were Paulie Principe and Frank Russo, the two sluggers who'd helped Tommy beat me to a pulp. Then I spotted Checko Brown, the Colombo soldier, talking to Fat Andy Ruggiano, the Gambino capo. Bobby DeSimone, fresh from a stint in the joint, was sitting next to T.A. I stopped in my tracks and started to tremble. I was frozen to the pavement. Tommy came hurrying over.

"Joey, don't worry, relax. Didn't I tell you we wasn't gonna do that no more? Come over here, say hello to the boys. Cook us some food, Joey. We're sick of this hotel ____."

We made small talk for a while, then Tommy asked me to make the boys lunch. But first, he added, why didn't I put on a swim suit. "I got an extra," he said. "It's hot out here, Joey. It'll be hotter over the stove. Checko, get Joey a suit."

It was an odd request. Checko was fully dressed. So was DeSimone. Nevertheless, Checko and I walked to the cabana and Checko found the suit. I got undressed in front of him. The only place a wire could have been was up my rear. Checko didn't check there. In the kitchen I started deveining the shrimp, watching Checko walk the fifteen paces or so back to the boys. When he reached them, the crew looked at me, then at Checko.

"*È pulito,*" Checko said. *He's clean.* What the hell? Did this moron think I didn't understand Italian? Forgive and forget, right, Tommy? Enjoy the scampi, boys. And don't choke on 'em.

Shrimp Scampi Gambino-Style

2 pounds shrimp (preferably under 15 to a pound)
¾ pound (3 sticks) butter, softened
3 shallots, chopped fine
4 cloves garlic, crushed and chopped fine
Juice of ½ lemon
2 tablespoons chopped fresh parsley
½ cup plain dry bread crumbs
1 egg yolk
1 teaspoon Accent (optional)
2 teaspoons Red Devil hot sauce
Salt and pepper to taste

Clean, devein, and butterfly shrimp. Place them in large, flat pan. Mix butter, shallots, garlic, lemon juice, parsley, bread crumbs, egg yolk, Accent, hot sauce, and salt and pepper to taste in bowl. Spoon over raw shrimp. Place under broiler for 3 to 5 minutes, checking occasionally so that they do not overcook. Spoon excess melted sauce over shrimp and serve. *Serves 5. Add more shrimp for more people.*

Over lunch, with me still in my bathing suit, everyone talked a little more freely and came a little closer to me—except Principe and Russo, who stayed in the pool. I'd made the right move not wearing the wire. Business could now commence.

Menu

Lobster Newburg

SINGER ISLAND, FLORIDA, 1982
MY NEW APARTMENT

PEOPLE PRESENT:
Joe Dogs
John Bonino (FBI agent, Joe's undercover partner)
Larry Doss
Gunnar Askland

J knew Agent John Bonino was going to make a good undercover partner when, over a delicious meal of veal and pasta marinara, I pulled my "chop you up and flush you down the toilet" routine on him and his only reply was to ask me what ingredients I put in my marinara sauce.

Bonino was out of the Eye's Chicago office, and the Feds in Washington were grubstaking us to an illegal after-hours club we'd use to sting the Florida mob. The bottle club was equipped with all kinds of surveillance cameras, and since I was now back in T.A.'s good graces, the Feds figured we'd pick up all kinds of good information. I passed John off as my money man—everyone knew I was broke since the beating—an old friend who wanted to get out of the drug-smuggling business and into a "legit" operation. The bottle club was the perfect cover.

I was cooking for Bonino, Agent Larry Doss, and Agent Gunnar Askland in my new apartment in a high-rise on Singer Island. The Feds had sprung for apartments for me and John in the same building. Over cocktails, I mentioned to the agents that I'd been coming out of my barbershop on the Island that afternoon when I'd seen a car drive through the parking lot. A wiseguy named Skeets was driving, Johnny Irish was in the front passenger's seat, and Tony Black was in the back. Nothing particularly odd. But there's nothing particularly odd about this special dish, either. Sweet lobster with a rich béchamel sauce. *Perfetto* for those quiet evenings at home with the Feds.

Lobster Newburg

3 tablespoons clarified butter, melted and clarified by
    pouring off milky sediment
½ teaspoon paprika
¼ cup cooking sherry
1 quart Béchamel Sauce (see page 89)
2 basil leaves
4 to 6 drops yellow food coloring
Pinch of salt
¼ teaspoon white pepper
1 teaspoon chicken base or 2–3 chicken bouillon cubes
    dissolved in ¼ cup water
1½ pounds lobster meat (Maine preferred)

*P*ut 2½ tablespoons clarified butter in medium saucepan and heat until bubbly (don't burn) over low flame. Add paprika and whisk vigorously. Add sherry, ignite, and cook alcohol off. When alcohol has evaporated, add béchamel sauce and stir until blended. Add basil leaves and simmer for 20 minutes (do not boil). Add food coloring, salt and pepper, and chicken base and simmer for additional 10 minutes, stirring occasionally. Remove basil leaves. Coat separate frying pan with remaining butter and sauté lobster meat, stirring constantly. When hot, remove lobster and add to sauce. Simmer for additional 5 minutes and serve with yellow rice or rice pilaf. *Serves 4.*

Midway through dinner the phone rang in my bedroom.

"Hello?" Out of habit I pushed the "record" button on my nightstand.

"I didn't think you were home. You usually get the phone on the first ring." It was Little Dom. Once I heard his voice I stopped the tape from recording.

Dom told me to expect an invitation to his son's upcoming wedding, and we were just making small talk when out of nowhere he asked cryptically, "My friend Johnny, down south there, you know who I mean?"

He meant Johnny Irish. "What about him?"

"He's gone, Joey. Gone."

"Are you kidding me, Dominick?"

"Hey, Joey! I don't joke about something like that. My *compare*, Donny Shacks, he told me about six o'clock tonight that he was gone."

"Dom, he's got to be mistaken," I said. "I saw him with Tony Black and Skeets, driving around Singer Island late this afternoon. Around four o'clock."

"Hey, Joe, what the ____ is wrong with you?" Dom said. "I don't give a ____ if you saw him at five-thirty. He's gone. *Capisci?*"

I hung up the phone, went back to the dining room, and announced to the Feds that Johnny Irish had been whacked. We all skipped dessert. And nobody was ever charged with Irish's murder.

Menu

Caponata

WEST PALM BEACH, FLORIDA, 1982
DON LUIGI'S RESTAURANT

PEOPLE PRESENT:
Joe Dogs
Tommy Agro
Fat Andy Ruggiano
Skinny Bobby DeSimone
Frank Russo
Paulie Principe

Tommy Agro showed up at Don Luigi's with the capo Fat Andy Ruggiano and the rest of his crew in tow. Bobby DeSimone. Paulie Principe and Frank Russo— the boys who, along with Tommy a few months earlier, had tried to shuffle me off this mortal coil. Don Luigi's was owned by Don Ritz, a member of my crew, and I felt pretty safe there. I was wearing a wire. At first T.A. didn't like having Ritz around because he thought he was Jewish. The mob is the most prejudiced group around, after all. But when I explained to Tommy that "Ritz" was a shortened Italian name, he cooled down.

Don Ritz got everyone seated in a private room in the rear of the restaurant and I headed off to the kitchen to prepare my famous caponata, one of Tommy's favorites. While I was cooking, Don Ritz, a stutterer, joined me. He looked nervous.

"Christ, Joe, I can't believe these guys," he stammered. "They come down here, beat you, leave you for dead, and then they want you to cook for them? I wou ... wou ... wou ... wouldn't do it."

I laughed to myself. Don was a real nice guy. He had a heart of gold and he ran a fine restaurant. All he wanted to do in life was make good pizzas.

"Yeah, Don, that's just how they are," I joked. "I hope they like the caponata, because they sure didn't like the fettuccine I made. They almost killed me over it."

"I don't know how you can joke around like that," Don said. "Don't you hate them?"

"Nah. Why should I hate them? By the way, Don, you got any arsenic around here? I'm going to kill the whole group."

"Joe, quit ____ing around," he said. "I just got this joint. I got a lot of money stuck in here. If you want to whack them, please do it somewhere else."

Don Ritz's stuttering became even more pronounced when Bobby DeSimone walked into the kitchen. "Joey, Joey," DeSimone said in that fag voice of his. "I was just telling Tommy that you make the best caponata I ever tasted. Can I watch?"

"I'm glad you like it, Bobby, but listen, this ain't my joint. So you can't hang around back here. You'll get in the chef's way."

As DeSimone walked back out, I said loud enough for him to hear, "Don, hand me that stuff I wanted to mix into the sauce."

You could almost see the light bulb going off over Skinny Bobby's head. He half turned, looked at me suspiciously, and continued out.

"Wh . . . wh . . . why did you say that?" Don stammered. "Now he's gonna tell them there's poison in the sauce."

"____ 'em, I said. "Let 'em sweat a little bit."

Caponata

¾ cup olive oil (extra-virgin or virgin preferred)
2 large onions, chopped into ¼-inch cubes
4 cloves garlic, smashed and chopped fine
½ pound prosciutto, sliced and cut into ½-inch pieces
2 slices bacon
2 cans jumbo black olives, pitted and sliced (each can
     5¾ oz. drained)
½ cup heavy cream
1½ pounds perciatelli pasta
1 cup freshly grated Parmesan cheese
3 egg yolks, beaten

*H*eat olive oil in large frying pan. Add onions and garlic and sauté until translucent. Add prosciutto and bacon and cook until bacon is crisp. Remove bacon and discard. Add olives and cook until very soft, stirring often. With a slotted spoon, remove all ingredients to a bowl and pour cream into olive oil. Whisk with wire whip until texture develops. Return all ingredients to pan. Sauce is finished. Keep hot. Meanwhile, pasta should be boiling. Cook it *al dente*. Drain, but do not rinse. Put pasta back in pot. Add Parmesan cheese, toss, and stir. Add egg yolks slowly, tossing pasta as you do so until pasta is thoroughly covered. Place on large platter, spoon sauce over pasta, and serve. *Serves 6.*

I spooned the sauce over the perciatelli and told Don to serve it to the crew while I washed up. He brought it out and three or four minutes later walked back into the kitchen smiling.

"They want you to eat with them," Don said without a stutter. "They're waiting for you before they start."

I walked out of the kitchen with a grin. "C'mon, fellas, dig in."

"After you," Fat Andy insisted. "Here, Joey, let me put some on a plate for you. I mean, after all, you did all the cooking and we want to show our appreciation. Honey? Honey, bring Joe Dogs a nice scotch. Dewar's, isn't it, Joe?"

Andy filled my dish and told me to dig in while he and the other guys filled their plates. I took a couple of healthy bites and licked my chops. Everyone stared.

"Aren't you guys going to eat?" I asked as I filled my mouth again. They started eating, and the compliments began rolling in.

Menu

Bracciole

NORTH MIAMI BEACH, FLORIDA, 1982
FAT ANDY RUGGIANO'S HOUSE

PEOPLE PRESENT:
Joe Dogs   John Bonino
Fat Andy Ruggiano   Sal Reale (Gambino soldier)
Ronnie "Stone" Pearlman
Junior "Fingers" Abbandando
and Gerry Alicino (Gambino associates)
Skinny Bobby DeSimone

*F*BI agent John Bonino—aka drug smuggler John Marino—and I were invited to the Gambino capo Fat Andy's house to pick up a $25,000 shylock loan. We'd told him we needed it to start our illegal gambling joint—disguised as a "bottle club"—in Riviera Beach. It would turn out to be the largest illegal loan ever taken by an undercover Fed from the Mafia, and John would get lots of awards for it. It would also be introduced as evidence, later, during Fat Andy's racketeering trial.

Fat Andy's crew met us in his driveway. There was Sal Reale, a made member in Fat Andy's gang. And Ronnie "Stone" Pearlman, who could only be an associate because he was a Jew. (The Mafia not being an equal-opportunity employer.) Junior "Fingers" Abbandando, who got a discount at the manicurist because he only had nine fingers, was there. Bobby DeSimone and Gerry Alicino were standing on the porch.

The crew had met John once, and they were at ease, so we talked about the club, the different prices for building materials, where to get blackjack and roulette tables, that kind of thing. John and I were both wearing Nagra body recorders.

After an hour, Fat Andy asked me to join him in the kitchen to whip up some grub. Sal Reale followed me in.

"Joe, just how well do you know this guy John?" Reale began. There was a menace to his voice. "We're giving him the loan only because of you. You understand that, don't you? Your friend T.A. said that you're tops with him. So that's why we're doing it."

"Well, if Tommy said all these nice things about me, what the _____ are we talking about here?" I bluffed, turning to Fat Andy. "Did you bring me in here to read me the riot act or to cook dinner? I feel insulted, Andy. Look, forget the loan. I'll get it for John somewhere else. See you at the club."

I turned for the door and felt a hand on my shoulder. I almost crapped in my pants. I was sweating so much I was afraid I'd short-circuit the Nagra. It was Fat Andy's paw.

"Joe, don't feel insulted." He was being conciliatory. "Sal didn't mean no harm. He just asked you one little question, that's all. Come on now, shake hands, and make us something nice to eat."

Sal and I shook hands, and laughed. *"Marrone,* what a hothead," he said as he tried to hand me the money.

"Sal, do me a favor," I said. "Give it to John. It'll make him feel respected if you were to hand it to him and make the arrangements about the vig."

"Okay, Joe. After dinner."

Braccole

¼ pound (1 stick) butter, melted
2 tablespoons olive oil (extra-virgin or virgin preferred)
8 (4-inch) pieces eye or bottom round steak, pounded
    thin with mallet
Salt and pepper to taste
4 cloves garlic, smashed and chopped fine
1 cup plain dry bread crumbs
½ cup chopped fresh parsley
4 hard-boiled eggs, chopped
Tomato Sauce (recipe on page 128)

*R*ub mixture of butter and oil into one side of each piece of meat. Rub salt and pepper into same side. Spread layer of chopped garlic over same side. Cover garlic with layer of bread crumbs. Cover bread crumbs with layer of parsley. Cover parsley with layer of chopped eggs. Roll and tie with sewing string (or secure with toothpicks). Fry over medium heat approximately 3 to 4 minutes until brown all over. Remove from frying pan and simmer in tomato sauce for 2 hours. *Serves 4.*

Over coffee Sal made a big show of handing John the money. Then they settled on the vig—a very reasonable two points a week. "Why choke the guy?" Fat Andy asked magnanimously. Little did he know who would eventually be choking on that loan.

Menu

Stuffed Shells
with Tomato Sauce

KEW GARDENS, QUEENS, NEW YORK, 1983
TOMMY AGRO'S HOUSE

PEOPLE PRESENT:
Joe Dogs
Tommy Agro
Tommy Agro's geisha girl

The phone was ringing as I walked into my hotel suite in Queens at eleven a.m., the morning after Sammy Cataldo's wedding—Sammy was Little Dom's kid. Tommy Agro was on the line, summoning me to his home.

Tommy had a beautiful mansion in Kew Gardens, Queens, with two marble fireplaces, including one in a master bedroom measuring one thousand square feet, and a spacious and spotless kitchen. Tommy's wife Marian was now his ex-wife, and T.A. kept the house stocked with a bevy of exotic broads. I was shown into the living room by a comely little geisha.

"Here's $1,200 for four weeks, Tip," I said, handing him his juice. "I know the last week isn't due yet, but since I'm up here you might as well take it."

"Yeah, thanks, Joey," he answered gruffly. "Let's throw together some lunch, and then we gotta talk." Something was definitely bothering him. Maybe my stuffed shells would soothe the savage beast. This is a three-part recipe—the meatballs for the tomato sauce, the sauce itself, and the cheese filling for the shells. It takes time but is definitely worth the wait and effort.

Stuffed Shells with Tomato Sauce

Meatballs

> 1 pound ground beef
> 1 small onion, diced
> 3 cloves garlic, smashed and chopped fine
> 1 egg
> ¼ cup ketchup
> ½ cup plain dry bread crumbs
> Salt and pepper to taste

*M*ix all ingredients together and form meatballs. Set aside.

Tomato Sauce

> 3 tablespoons corn oil
> Meatballs (recipe above)
> 1 pound sausage, cut into 3-inch pieces
> 2 (28-ounce) cans peeled tomatoes (Progresso Pomodori
>   Pelati con Basilico preferred), crushed
> 1 cup chicken stock
> 2 (6-ounce) cans tomato paste
> 2 cups water (or chicken stock)
> Salt and pepper to taste

*H*eat oil in pot over low flame. Sauté meatballs and sausage, turning occasionally, until browned (turn gently, so as not to break meatballs). Add tomatoes and cook over low heat for 45 minutes, stirring occasionally. Once tomatoes have cooked, add chicken stock, tomato paste, and 2 cups water (or additional chicken stock). Stir gently to blend. Add salt and pepper to taste, and cook for 4 hours on low flame.

⌇⌇

SHELLS AND FILLING

> *1 pound jumbo shells*
> *3 cups whole-milk ricotta cheese (Polly-O brand pre-*
> *ferred)*
> *½ pound mozzarella cheese, diced*
> *3 eggs*
> *2 tablespoons chopped fresh parsley*
> *Salt and pepper to taste*
> *⅓ cup freshly grated Parmesan cheese*

*B*oil shells, drain, and run cold water over them. Mix ricotta, mozzarella, eggs, parsley, and salt and pepper in bowl. Put filling into each shell. Place thin layer of tomato sauce along bottom of baking pan. Place shells on top of layer of sauce and pour remaining sauce over shells. Sprinkle grated Parmesan over everything. Cover with foil and bake in preheated 350-degree oven for 15 to 20 minutes. *Serves 4 to 6.*

As it turned out, this was one fabulous culinary creation that I never did get to eat . . . at least not that day at Tommy's house. For while the sauce was simmering, T.A. started fulminating.

"Listen, Joey, who's this guy you brought up here with you?"

"He's a good friend," I answered. "Name's John Marino. From Chicago. And I know him longer than I know you. What's on your mind, Tip?"

"What's on my mind is you're sure he's all right? I mean, you don't have any illusions that you think you can bring a cop around here to try and get in with us, do you, Joey?" I had to hand it to T.A. His instincts were good, and sometimes he wasn't as dumb as he looked.

"Look, Tom, in all due respect, I didn't come here to be insulted, all right?" I said. "I told you who he was. If you'd like to check him out, be my guest. It would give me great pleasure to get an apology from you. John is my partner in the *babonia*. I earn off the guy." *Babonia* was our word for drugs.

"So this guy's your dope partner, huh?" Tommy growled. "Well, let me tell you something, Joey, and I'm only gonna tell you once. The boss, Big Paulie, he's put out the word. No more drugs. He just had three made guys from Neil's side of the *famiglia* whacked for dealing in that ____. They were all with that c____er Gotti's crew."

T.A. was rolling now, as only T.A. could when he worked himself up into one of his apoplectic fits. His face was purple. The words were bursting out of his mouth at the top of his lungs. It was a good time to look for a place to hide. I saw none.

"So, Pippie, don't make me have to tell you no more. Understand? Find some other way to earn. And if that guy John continues to do it, you're going to have to answer for him. So tell him. *Finito! Capisci?* Don't let me find out different.

"And don't bring him around me. I don't want to meet him. Fat Andy likes him? That's fine. Put him with Andy. But you belong here, Joey, *capisci?* You aren't going anywhere. But tell that guy John if he ____s with drugs, he's going bye-bye and you're the one who's gonna send him off.

"Now get out of here. You make me lose my appetite. Go back to Florida and earn. Send me some money, you hump."

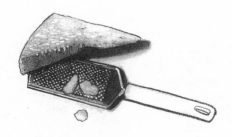

Menu

Bouillabaisse

SINGER ISLAND, FLORIDA, 1983
MY APARTMENT

PEOPLE PRESENT:
Joe Dogs
John Bonino
Robbie (Colombo associate)

hree days after Christmas Robbie called. Robbie hung around Freddie Campo—one of the biggest bookmakers in south Florida. As part of the FBI sting operation, I was splitting a bookmaking halfsheet with him. John Bonino, the undercover, had all the agents calling in and making football bets, for evidence. Anyway, I'd told John that a few years earlier, Robbie had called me one day around three in the morning and said that a local lob named Stanley Gerstenfeld had been whacked. Stanley was a tough-guy wannabe and degenerate gambler. The State's Attorney had called me in for questioning about Stanley's murder because I'd brained Stanley in a local saloon a few weeks before he was capped, but I had an airtight alibi. The murder was still listed as "unsolved" on the Florida books.

At any rate, Robbie was the writer and collector on our bookmaking sheet, and it was time for our weekly payoff meeting. John told me to ask Robbie over for dinner and try to get him to open up about Stanley's murder. Robbie was an egomaniac, and I figured it wouldn't be too hard to pull his chain. He was in a good mood when he arrived, and after he paid me my vig I opened a bottle of scotch. John and Robbie made small talk while I threw dinner together. A nice fish stew for someone who someday may sleep with the fishes.

Bouillabaisse

¼ cup olive oil (extra-virgin or virgin preferred)
10 to 15 live blue crabs (quickly pre-boiled and cleaned)
3 cloves garlic, smashed and chopped
½ pound squid
1 pound shrimp (25 to 30)
12 to 15 clams
12 to 15 mussels
1 pound any nonoily fish (optional)
2 (28-ounce) cans Italian tomatoes (Progresso
*   Pomodori Pelati con Basilico preferred)*
1 pound linguine
Salt and pepper to taste

*H*eat olive oil in large pot. Place crabs and garlic in pot and toss or stir for 10 minutes. Place lid over pot and simmer for another 10 minutes. Add all other ingredients—except pasta—and cook over medium flame for 30 minutes, stirring often. Boil pasta, drain, and pour bouillabaisse over pasta. *Serves 4.*

As we were eating and talking, I brought up the subject of the late Stanley Gerstenfeld. "You know, Robbie," I said, "Stanley had a hunch that something was wrong, because before he died he kept trying to reach me. In fact, he did reach me, and wanted to talk to me, but we never got together. I think he knew what was coming."

"He didn't know a ____ing thing," Robbie spat out, like a true tough guy. "When I put the bag over his head, *then* he knew he was going. I put three or four in his head, and one in his heart so he wouldn't bleed all over the car."

"Oh, does that stop the bleeding?" I asked, playing dumb.

"Yeah, Joey. You're putting me on. You know it does."

This entire conversation took place right in front of John, who did the right thing by sitting there nice and quiet, just listening and letting that little Nagra tape recorder roll under his shirt. We got the whole thing on tape. But the authorities never went after Robbie—maybe it was just a good story. Who knows?

After Robbie left I mentioned to John that, deep down, Robbie was nothing less than a maniac. "Did you hear him say he wishes he was Italian?"

"More Italians like him we don't need," John answered. "We need some nice quiet ones, like your pal Tommy A."

Menu

Veal Oscar

HALLANDALE, FLORIDA, 1983
TOMMY AGRO'S HOTEL SUITE

PEOPLE PRESENT:
Joe Dogs
Tommy Agro
two Chinese hookers

ommy called at the end of January. He was down south in his suite at the Dip, and he wanted me pronto. He had two Chinese hookers with him and he needed me to cook dinner. What began as an ordinary evening—I didn't wear a wire that night; too dangerous—ended in an epiphany. But first we ate. Tommy had the hotel's kitchen send up everything I needed for my four-star Veal Oscar with hollandaise sauce.

Veal Oscar

4 veal cutlets
2 tablespoons olive oil (extra-virgin or virgin preferred)
2 (8-ounce) cans crabmeat
1 bunch fresh spinach, stemmed, washed, and steamed
Hollandaise Sauce (recipe on page 47)

auté veal in olive oil in frying pan approximately 2 minutes each side. Remove crabmeat from can and layer over veal. Layer spinach over crabmeat. Bake for 5 minutes in preheated 350-degree oven. Remove, place in serving dish, spoon hollandaise sauce over top, and serve.

After dinner, Tommy handed the hookers a roll of cash and sent them down to the hotel's shopping arcade. He had business to discuss. I'll never forget the conversation that followed.

"Listen, you _____in' suitcase, there's something I want to tell you," he barked in that soft-spoken manner of his. "But you have to promise me that it doesn't go any further than this room. Because if it does, it'll make me look bad, and I'll have a bad taste in my mouth."

"Who would I tell?" I asked, throwing up my hands and cursing myself for not wearing the Nagra.

T.A.'s face turned serious. "Joey, I didn't want to hurt you the way I did," he said. "It wasn't my fault. My *compare*, Joe Gallo, made me do it. It wasn't me, or the money you owed me. He just used that as an excuse to get to you. I swear, Joey. It wasn't me."

I was stunned. "But why would Gallo want to hurt me? After all the money he made with us on the dope? On the racetrack scam? And what about the beating I gave that guy up in Naples because of his little _____ing bitch? The guy whose sister he was dating, the one who didn't want him around?"

"Stop, Joey! Stop right there! I told you once before never to talk like that about my *compare*. Besides, that's the reason. That guy you _____ed up, the zip with the sister. You _____ed him up too much. You wasn't supposed to hurt him that bad. That girl, Sophia, she left my *compare* over that. It's been eating at him ever since, and he blames you."

I was flabbergasted. I'd been maimed, I'd almost been killed, I'd gone to work for the Feds, all because of Joe Gallo's little bitch on the side! It couldn't be. Tommy had to be lying.

After a long pause, T.A. continued. "What can I say, Joey? Except that my *compare* wanted you *morto*. It's a good thing Don

Ritz's wife walked in or right now you'd either be dead, or with no right hand."

"You should have shot me, Tommy," I cried. It wasn't an act. "You should have killed me. I didn't deserve to be left like that. I've been nothing but loyal to you for over ten years. And look at me. I'm ____ed up! I look like a freak! I can't even eat without cocking my head. I don't even feel the liquor I'm drinking. I got a lump on my forehead the size of an orange. All this because Joe Gallo blames me for losing his little ____? A man would have killed me, Tommy. A man wouldn't have left me like this."

For once Tommy Agro was speechless. He just stood there shrugging his shoulders. I wheeled and stalked out of the room. I didn't feel like a hooker that night. Not even a Chinese one.

Menu

Maine Lobster Fra Diavolo
Lemon Granita

HALLANDALE, FLORIDA, 1983
TOMMY AGRO'S HOTEL CABANA

PEOPLE PRESENT:
Joe Dogs
Tommy Agro
Skinny Bobby DeSimone

*J*oey, I'm down here at the Dip. Bobby's with me. Meet me by the pool. I got to see you about my *compare*'s thing." T.A. sounded calm.

It had been two months since Tommy'd informed me that I'd nearly been beaten to death on orders from his *compare*, the Gambino family *consigliere* Joe N. Gallo. Ever since, I'd been burning with revenge to nail both of those bastards. Luckily, fortune struck. My Colombo *famiglia* pal Little Dom Cataldo had gone away on an armed-robbery beef, but before he went in he asked if I had any connections to get him an easy prison stretch at one of the federal country clubs. Dom had made the request because he knew my girlfriend Nena's father was a big muckety-muck in Washington, D.C. But, instead, I'd taken Dom's request to my new associates in the Eye, and they'd arranged for Little Dom to do his time at Allenwood Federal Penitentiary, the crème de la crème of soft time.

The Feds were hoping that Dom would spread the word throughout the mob that Joe Dogs could fix prison sentences, thereby enabling them to build a racketeering case against anyone who bit. Their plan worked like a charm. No sooner was Dom plunked down in Allenwood than the Colombos had me make similar arrangements for Carmine "the Snake" Persico, who wanted to serve his time close to New York. For $20,000, my "connection" would arrange it. And then Tommy Agro called me about Joe Gallo's kid, who was doing hard time in Attica, a snake pit in upstate New York. Gallo wanted his son transferred to a softer pen, and, per the FBI's instructions, I played along with the sting. This offshoot of Operation Home Run came to be known as the Favors case. There was only one problem. The Colombo organization had failed at first to come up with the scratch for the Snake, and the Feds, pissed off that no money had changed hands, had had Dom transferred to Kentucky, where he was doing hard time. I felt bad about that.

T.A. and Skinny Bobby were drinking coffee by the cabana when I arrived at the Diplomat Hotel. T.A. thought I was pulling prison strings through Nena's connection in Washington. His boss, Gallo, had arranged to get his kid transferred out of Attica for $20,000.

"Bobby's got the money in the hotel safe," Agro began. "Tell your friend in Washington we got the bread, but it stays right here until my *compare*'s kid is moved. Now, make us some lunch."

Maine Lobster Fra Diavolo

¼ *cup olive oil*

3 *Maine lobsters 1¼–1½ pounds each, split in half and claws cracked*

4 *cloves garlic, crushed and sliced paper-thin with razor blade*

1 *(28-ounce) can Italian tomatoes (Progresso Pomodori Pelati con Basilico preferred), crushed*

3 *to 4 fresh basil leaves*

Half (28-ounce) can fish stock (or water)

1 *pound linguine*

*H*eat olive oil in extra-large frying pan. Place split lobsters, cracked claws, and their juice in pan. Sauté for 5 minutes over medium heat, adding garlic as you turn lobsters. Add tomatoes, basil leaves, and fish stock (or water), cover, and simmer for approximately 12 minutes. Season to taste. Boil pasta (*al dente* is best), drain, and spoon lobster and sauce over individual servings. Goes best with a nice red chianti or burgundy. *Serves 3.*

⌇⌇⌇

T.A. ate lobster like he did everything else. Like a pig. The guy needed a half-dozen bibs. During dinner the Nagra was pressing against my balls and killing me. I'd taken to wearing the tape recorder in my crotch—as opposed to my chest or back, because no true wiseguy would ever grab your ____. But after this conversation, I was glad I had it on.

"I feel so bad about Dominick," I told Tommy. "He's terrified of them big bad black guys in his cell block. And another thing, my connection in Washington is leery since he didn't get the money yet for the Snake. We got to make sure we do the right thing on Gallo's kid. *Capisci?*"

"Don't you worry, Joey, didn't I just tell you we got the money right here? You want to see it? You asking me to prove it to you?" I felt an Agro rampage coming on. "And another thing, my friend, if I was you, I wouldn't be worrying so much about the health of your great good friend Dominick Cataldo. Maybe he ain't as friendly as you think. Do you think I should tell him, Bobby?"

"Yeah, Tommy, I think you should tell him," DeSimone squeaked.

"What? What?" I asked. "Tell me what?"

"Tell you that your good friend Little Dom put a contract out on you," T.A. yelled. He let the words hang in the air for a moment. "Dom was taking credit for having the jailhouse juice. Then, when he got moved, it made him look bad with his *famiglia*. He wanted you dead. The guy Dom got to whack you came to my people for the okay, so we put a squash on it at a sit-down. So how do you feel about your good friend Little Dom Cataldo now?"

I was pretty shaken. But, truthfully, I also felt real good that the Nagra was rolling in my pants. It took me a minute to catch my breath. So Dom wanted me capped, huh? Well, ____ Little Dominick Cataldo. ____ him and the horse he rode in on. It was true. The Mafia has no friends, only interests. In that case I was going to enjoy my dessert.

<section break>

Lemon Granita

½ cup sugar
2 cups water
6 to 7 lemons (enough for 1 cup of juice)

Make a syrup by mixing sugar and water in pot, bringing mixture to boil over medium flame, and boiling for 5 minutes. Turn off flame and allow syrup to reach room temperature. Mix with lemon juice and freeze in cups or pony glasses. (*Note:* the freezing process will take about an hour more than making ice because of the sugar content.) *Serves 3.*

Menu

Crabmeat Appetizers
Steaks Cognac

CAPE CORAL, FLORIDA, 1983
AN FBI SAFE HOUSE

PEOPLE PRESENT:
Joe Dogs
Larry Doss
Dick Gentlecore (FBI agent)
Roma Theus (Federal Prosecutor)

By August of 1983 it was all over. Operation Home Run had closed down. Word had leaked to the Mafia from several sources—including one from the FBI's Washington headquarters—that someone in Florida was cooperating with the Eye. It didn't take a brain surgeon to figure out who that "someone" was. A third contract was put out on me. It was an "open" contract—anyone could collect. I don't know how much it was for.

Right before we closed down I'd flown to New York for one last sitdown with Tommy Agro. We'd met at a bar near the airport. The agents hadn't wanted me to go, but I insisted. Turned out to be a circus. The joint was crawling with mobsters and undercover Feds, who were very hard to pick out with their wingtips and white socks. Even Tommy had to laugh, after he'd had Fat Andy frisk me for a wire. I wasn't wearing the Nagra that night. No matter. T.A. knew. They all knew. I think they'd planned to cap me right there. But there were just too many cops in the joint. Before I left, Tommy told me he'd get me, whatever it took. Reach up from the grave if he had to, he said. He wasn't kidding.

So the Government moved me to a safe house in Cape Coral, at the ass end of the world. And the only thing I had to look forward to was waiting to testify at the trials of all my old friends and cooking for the Feds during our strategy sessions. I had plenty of time to experiment in the kitchen. On one rainy Saturday, I was visited by agents Larry Doss, Dick Gentlecore, and Federal Prosecutor Roma Theus, who would be prosecuting the first case. I decided to do up something extra special, just in case this was *my* last supper.

Crabmeat Appetizers

¼ pound (1 stick) butter, softened
1 jar Kraft Old English cheese
1½ teaspoons mayonnaise
½ teaspoon garlic salt
½ teaspoon Cavander's (Greek seasoning)
8 ounces crabmeat
6 English muffins (12 halves, toasted)

*M*elt butter in pan. (Do not burn!) Stir in rest of ingredients (excluding muffins), being careful not to overmix and break up crabmeat too much. Spread mixture generously over English muffins and bake in preheated 350-degree oven approximately 5 to 8 minutes. Broil for a few seconds to brown tops, cut into quarters, and serve. *Makes 48.*

"Great crab puffs, they got a nice bite to them," said Roma Theus, opening up his briefcase. "Now, Joe, here's a list of all the shylock payments you made to Tommy A. during the investigation. You have to study them and try to remember them. Dates, places, and amounts. You're going to be asked about them on the stand."

I rolled my eyes at these guys. My brain ain't built for that kind of thing.

"You can do it, Joe," piped up Larry Doss. "Pay attention to Roma here. He's the real deal. Graduate of Harvard, Phi Beta Kappa, number three in his class. He's intelligent, Joe, and he's going to help you."

"Gee, Larry, that's terrific, Roma being all those things," I said. "But, hey, my father was a bookmaker, and you don't hear me bragging about it." Then I went into the kitchen to cook the steaks.

Steaks Cognac

4 filets mignons, 8 ounces each
3 tablespoons olive oil (extra-virgin or virgin preferred)
2 onions, chopped
8 large mushrooms, cleaned and sliced
½ cup beef stock
¼ cup cognac (Rémy Martin preferred)
Salt and pepper to taste

*S*auté steaks to desired doneness in olive oil. Remove from frying pan and set aside. Add onions and mushrooms to steak drippings (add a little more olive oil, if needed). Sauté until almost done, approximately 8 to 10 minutes, then add beef stock, cognac, and salt and pepper to taste. Ignite to cook off alcohol. Simmer until mixture is reduced to half. Reheat steaks in sauce and serve with vegetables and baked potato. (*Note:* Asparagus Hollandaise, on page 47, also goes well with this dish.) *Serves 4.*

After dinner, Larry Doss made sure I had four or five scotches in me before he broke the news. I thought everybody was being just a little too nice.

"Joe, we got a problem," the agent began. "Indictments were handed up in New York this week, and it looks like there was a leak. We went to pick up Fat Andy, but he hasn't been home in days. His crew was scattered, too. It gets worse, Joe, and I know you're not going to like this. Tommy Agro's blown New York. He's in the wind. And we have no idea where he's hiding."

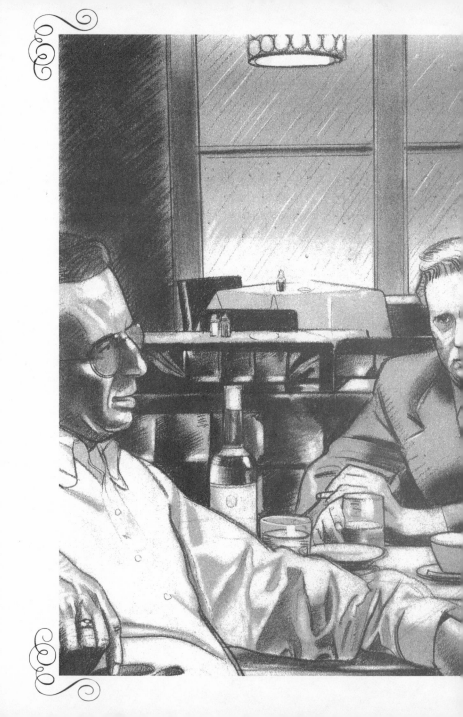

Minestrone

PORT CHARLOTTE, FLORIDA, 1985
ANOTHER FBI SAFE HOUSE

PEOPLE PRESENT:
Joe Dogs
Larry Doss
Peter Outerbridge (Federal Prosecutor)

*A*gent Larry Doss flew through the door of the safe house just as I was convincing this little babydoll waitress I'd met the night before to come and visit me. Peter Outerbridge, a Federal Prosecutor, was right behind him.

"Break out the Dewar's, Joe," Doss cried. "We nailed Tommy Agro in Montreal. You have to see that dumb little midget. He grew a mustache and thought no one would recognize him. The Royal Canadian Mounted Police picked him up for us."

"But how'd you get him back in the country?" I asked. "Ain't there a lot of red tape about crossing borders?"

"Plenty," said Doss. "Let's just say we cut a few corners and he was walked over the bridge—and into our waiting arms—up in Niagara Falls. Peter here's ready to bring him to trial."

This was the best news I'd heard in a long time, and it called for a special feast. Unfortunately, I hadn't planned on cooking. But there was enough stuff laying around the apartment for me to throw together a delicious minestrone

Minestrone

¼ cup olive oil (extra-virgin or virgin preferred)
2 to 3 cloves garlic, smashed and chopped fine
1 onion, chopped fine
½ cup sliced mushrooms
4 cups finely chopped fresh tomatoes (or 1 16-ounce can
    crushed tomatoes with juice; or 1 6-ounce can
    tomato paste with 3 cups vegetable stock)
½ cup chopped Italian (flat-leaf) parsley
2 bay leaves
1 teaspoon crushed dried oregano
2 teaspoons basil (preferably fresh, chopped)
½ teaspoon dried rosemary
1 cup precooked or canned beans (kidney, garbanzo,
    lima, pinto, or any combination of those. Note:
    garbanzo and kidney make a good combo!)
½ cup pasta (elbows, small shells, or broken spaghetti)
1 cup chopped celery
2 carrots, chopped
1 large potato, peeled and diced
1 green pepper, seeded and chopped
1 large zucchini, chopped
¾ cup green beans
10 to 12 broccoli florets

¼ cup fresh peas (or ½ package frozen peas)
¼ cup fresh corn kernels (or ½ package frozen corn)
1 small bunch fresh escarole, chopped
1½ quarts cooking water, approximately
Freshly grated Parmesan cheese
Salt and pepper to taste

Sauté garlic, onion, and mushrooms in oil until soft (add mushrooms last, as they cook quicker). Add tomatoes or tomato paste and stock, parsley and seasonings and simmer for approximately 30 minutes. Add beans and pasta, and continue simmering. In another pot, cook (or steam) chopped vegetables in ½ cup water until nearly done, approximately 5 to 7 minutes. Combine all vegetables, including cooking water, with soup. Add additional 1½ quarts cooking water. Add escarole 5 to 10 minutes before serving (escarole cooks very quickly and will reduce to a fraction of its original volume). Sprinkle each serving with Parmesan cheese. Serve with a good crusty bread and many Dewar's if your chief antagonist on the face of the earth has just been arrested. *Serves 8 or more.*

Between 1982 and 1991 I testified in twelve trials in Florida and New York, putting away many of the guys I worked with in the Mafia. It was Tommy Agro's turn to come to court in Florida in 1986 on charges of loansharking, extortion, and attempted murder, and the judge kept yelling at me for smiling at him throughout the whole trial. T.A. was sentenced to fifteen years, but he was let out early to go home and die of lung cancer, which he did, in June of '87. As for the other guys who accompanied T.A. to my beating, Paulie Principe was acquitted by the jury and Frank Russo was indicted but never arrested.

Since then, I have been asked by several people, mostly Feds, if, knowing what I know now, I'd ever do it again. It's a tough question. Some nights, after sitting in that witness stand putting my old pals away, I went back to my room and cried. It was never my intention to break everybody, to _____ everything up.

I only wanted revenge. Revenge on T.A. and, later, on his *compare* Joe N. Gallo. Well, I got my revenge. Gallo was sentenced to ten years. T.A. died. And now I'm stuck in the Witness Protection Program, being taken to dinner out in the middle of wahoo land by U.S. Marshals in joints that advertise "Italian Night" and then serve _____ing macaroni and ketchup instead of pasta. I guess it serves me right. *Capisci?*